AIR WAR OVER KOSOVO

Series Title

Military History

Air War Over Kosovo

Operational and Logistical Issues of the Air Campaign

Dr. Albert Atkins

Writers Club Press

San Jose New York Lincoln Shanghai

Air War Over Kosovo
Operational and Logistical Issues of the Air Campaign

Writers Club Press
an imprint of iUniverse.com, Inc.

For information address:
iUniverse.com, Inc.
620 North 48th Street, Suite 201
Lincoln, NE 68504-3467
www.iuniverse.com

ISBN: 0-595-13660-5

Printed in the United States of America

To the men and women of the United States Armed Forces

Epigraph

Our military objective is to degrade and damage the military and security structure that President Milosevic (Yugoslavian President) has used to depopulate and destroy the Albanian majority in Kosovo.

William S. Cohen, Secretary of Defense, to the Senate Armed Services Committee, 15 April, 1999

Contents

Acknowledgements

In a work of synthesis, such as this, the author owes thanks to many writers, too numerous to mention individually. The spot reference will indicate the author's indebtedness and tell from whose researching he has borrowed. Very special thanks are due to Colonel Holshousher, Commander of the 452nd Air Refueling Wing, USAFR and Colonel "Putt" Richards Commander of the 163rd Air Refueling Wing, ANG for so generously granting the author personal interviews and inside knowledge of Operation Allied Force over Kosovo adding invaluable factual data to this book.

The author also wants to thank Mr. Anthony H. Cordesman, Senior Fellow for Strategic Assessment of the Center for Strategic and International Studies for providing accurate and complete insight of the bombing campaign. And all the Air Force's commands the Air Combat Command and the Air Mobility Command for their valuable input. A special thanks is given to Brigadier General James R. McCarthy, USAF Ret. In providing encouragement, support and guidance to this work.

Introduction

History teaches us that there are countries in the world where political citizenship doesn't really account for anything, it is their ethnic background that matters.

The IRA bombs and terrorizes *Northern Ireland* where *British* are settled, *Basques* sabotage *Spanish* police stations claiming for their own piece of land. White and blacks squabble over who owns the land in a post-apartheid South Africa, and even in a well socialized *Canada*, *French* speaking separatists are claiming *Quebec* as an independent state from the rest of *Canada*. But in the *Balkans,* the story is somewhat different when two ethnic groups fight against each other for their own way of life. Mainly *Bosnia, Serbia* and *Croatia* compose the *Balkans* region. This region was the center of attention for the whole world, especially *Europe* and the U.S. for the 1990's and quite possible well into the 21st century.

From the news broadcasts, one heard the term *"Balkanization",* according to Terence Nelson, *ABC News (1999),* was coined back in 1912, amid similar chaos terrifies the industrialized world. Anytime a civil war starts, monetary and inflationary crises as well as regional tension among neighbours take place. Tensions among neighbours lead to seeking alliances. One can certainly remember the series of events that led to *World War I,* one little incident and the world was at war overnight.

Ethnic divisions in *Bosnia* remain strong. The *Muslim* government did not allowed displaced *Serbs* to return home, and *Croatian* and *Serbian* government officials return the favour by leaving millions with nothing from a peaceful settlement. *Serbs* regard *Kosovo* as an integral part of their Nation's history. The region is mainly the heart of *Serbian* national folklore and the battleground of the 1389 defeat of the medieval *Serbs* heroes by the *Ottoman Empire*, now Turkey. This in fact is the key event in their national pride. But, since 1389 up to date, the population of *Serbia* changed dramatically. During the *Turkish* domination, a continuous immigration of ethnic *Albanians* formed a permanent settlement in *Kosovo*. This owing to a *Serb* exodus and a higher *Albanian* birth rate. As of 1999, *Kosovo* is 90% *Albanian* majority.

In 1974, the Yugoslavian constitution gave *Kosovo* autonomy allowing Albanian language in schools, observing *Islamic* holly days and giving province representation in the old federal presidency. But in the late eighties, and foreseeing the break-up of the former *Soviet Union*, Slobodan Milosevic, used the *Kosovo* situation as a stepping stone into political power in *Serbia*. In 1989, president Milosevic moved quickly to remove *Kosovo's* autonomous status and deployed large numbers of *Serbian* police and troops to enforce it. Thus, declaring the *Albanian* language unofficial and changing the school curricula. One can certainly draw similarities in the way *Adolf Hitler* dealt with *Polish Jews* in 1939-1940. Thus, Milosevic actions led to a frantic opposition by *Albanians* of official institution and services and the creation of a parallel government in *Kosovo*, all this with its own health, taxation and educational systems.

Since 1997, tension in the *Balkans* region escalated, mainly provoked by the emergence of the Kosovo Liberation Army created in 1996. The *KLA* received momentum by the neighbouring *Albania's* policies of not favouring change through violent means and from Ibrahim Rugova, *Albania's* president, to gain any concessions from President Milosevic. The *KLA* is believed to be financially supported by *Albanians* living in the exile in *Germany* and *Switzerland* using arms smuggled from *Albania.*

This sort of actions led Slobodan Milosevic to a major crackdown in *Kosovo*. Such crackdown increased acts of violence of *Serbian Forces* to such an extend that caused 2 million ethnic Albanians to be expelled from Kosovo, suffering in the process, the burning of populated villages and indiscriminate killing of innocent civilians. It was called *"ethnic cleansing"* by Slobodan Milosevic.

Fearing the possibility of escalation of hostilities in the *Balkans,* the same region in which *World War I* started, the NATO-Clinton administration developed a policy toward *Kosovo* that can be summarized in just words…*"ambitious objectives, modest means"*…According to *Richard N. Haas,* Director of Foreign Policy Studies, *Washington Post* in his April 1999 report stated that:

"The goals are oft-stated and well known. An end to all acts of violence by Serbian forces; the return of 2 million of the people of Kosovo to their homes and the reestablishment of political autonomy; the insertion of an international force to provide security; and the withdrawal of all Serbian security forces from the province."

In order to achieve these goals, the Clinton-NATO administration opted for aerial attacks as a mean to an end. These means consisted of intensive and continuous aerial attacks on *Serbia* and *Serbian* forces in and throughout *Kosovo*. After two and one-half months of sustained aerial bombardment, Slobodan Milosevic pulled out from *Kosovo* and *NATO* forces from *Great Britain, Germany, France, United States* and *Russia* occupied *Kosovo* to restore peace and allow *Albanian* refugees to return.

But, *Operation Allied Force* may have taught NATO's European allies more than they wanted to know about U.S. capabilities and their own dependence on it in time of war, according to several Pentagon and European officials *(Aerospace Daily, August 17, 1999).*

Was NATO and the U.S. ready for *Operation Allied Force?* Was the campaign successful? The following is an impartial analysis of the 78-day air campaign covering military capabilities and logistics affecting its outcome.

Allied Forces Southern Europe

Operation Allied Force

Background

Operation *Allied Force* was major NATO contingency response focused at ensuring *Serbian* forces full compliance with *UN Security Resolution 1199* dated September 23, 1998. The military operation was part of NATO's actions to promote regional stability, cooperation and security, in support of the international community.

…An Allied Force in support of a peaceful resolution of the Kosovo crisis… pio@afsouth.nato.int

The first phase of this multinational operation was initiated on October 13, 1998. That was the day in which NATO's higher decision-making body, the North Atlantic Council, authorized an activation order allowing for both "limited air strikes" and a "phased air campaign" in the *Federal Republic of Yugoslavia,* should *Yugoslavian* authorities refuse to comply with the UN resolution. The execution of this air strike option was initially set to begin not earlier than 96 hours from the authorization of the activation order, to allow time for negotiations between Ambassador Holbrooke and *Federal Republic of Yugoslavia's* President Slobodan Milosevic to bear fruit, according to NATO officials. Progress in the diplomatic negotiations was largely due to steady pressure maintained by the alliance through deployment of NATO air and naval forces stationed in *Italy* and in the

Adriatic Sea. After nine days of steady negotiations, Ambassador Holbrooke secured a flimsy agreement from Mr. Milosevic to comply with the provisions of UN Security Council Resolution *(UNSCR) 1199*, with both air and ground regimes to verify compliance. In accordance with this agreement, signed on October 15, 1998, Mr. Milosevic committed to cease hostilities and withdraw mobilized forces in *Kosovo*. Furthermore, the agreement allows the international community to verify compliance by all parties with the provisions of UNSC *Resolution 1199*. This deployment was to be conducted through NATO unarmed flights and the deployment in *Kosovo* of a verification mission provided by the Organization for Security and Cooperation in Europe *(OSCE)*.

According to Department of Defense sources, as the 96-hour deadline for compliance with the negotiated settlement approached, the international community had clear evidence that Slobodan Milosovic was still far from complying with all the terms of the accord. As diplomatic efforts continued to secure full compliance, NATO officials decided to extend the period before the execution of air strikes would begin. NATO's extension gave Mr. Milosevic until October 27, 1998, to an unconditional compliance with *UNSCR 1199*. Based on briefings given at the Department of Defense, NATO additionally decided to maintain its readiness to launch air operations against the *Federal Republic of Yugoslavia* and to include continuing deployment of substantial air forces in the region. Just prior to the end of this extension on October 27, supporting evidence indicated that *Serbian* military and security forces made progress toward the demanded restrain and withdrawal. In spite of the substantial steps, NATO's objective remained in place to achieve *USNC* resolutions. Thus, NATO decided to maintain both activation orders in place, with its execution subjected to approval by the North Atlantic Council.

But, despite the progress made, the crisis was not over, NATO remained ready to act. The North Atlantic Council kept the situation in *Kosovo* under constant review. The activation of orders *(ACTODS)* for limited air operations and for phased air campaign remained in effect. NATO military forces remained prepared to carry out air operations should they be necessary. In the mean time, NATO's focus was on ensuring the effectiveness of the verification regime with *Operation Eagle Eye*.

It was evident that by March 23, 1999, all efforts to achieve a negotiated, political solution to the *Kosovo* crisis failed. There was no other alternative but to take military action. NATO's Secretary General Javier Solana directed the Supreme Allied Commander Europe *(SACEUR)* to commence military air operations against the *Federal Republic of Yugoslavia*. Thus, air operations commenced on March 24, 1999 under the nickname *"Operation Allied Force"*. The Supreme Allied Commander Europe *(SACEUR)* delegated authority for the implementation of *Operation Allied Force* to the Commander in Chief of Allied Forces Southern Europe *(CINCSOUTH)*, whose headquarters are located in Naples, Italy. *CINCSOUTH* delegated control of the operation to the Commander, Allied Air Forces Southern Europe *(COMAIRSOUTH)*, also based in Naples. Operational conduct of day-to-day missions was delegated to the commander 5th Allied Tactical Air Force, at Vicenza, Italy.

The mission of NATO *Operation Allied Force* was to implement one or several courses of action, either to conduct limited air operations, such as air strikes against designated military significant targets and/or to conduct a phased air campaign.

On June 9, 1999, while the air campaign was in its 78th day, NATO and *Yugoslavian* military authorities signed a Military Technical Agreement. The agreement specified the modalities and procedures for the full withdrawal of *Serbian Security Forces* from *Kosovo*. And, on June 10, 1999 NATO's Secretary General Javier Solana, having received reports indicating that the withdrawal of the *Serbian Security Forces* was in progress, directed air operations to be suspended. On June 20, 1999, after all *Serbian* military and police forces *(VJ/MUP)* had departed

Kosovo in compliance with the Military Technical Agreement *(MTA)* signed by the Commander of *KFOR* and terminate the air Campaign. Tentatively, part of the aircraft deployed to conduct *Allied Force* was eventually authorized to return to home bases. *(Adapted from transcripts of briefings given at the Department of Defense, Washington).*

Chapter I
Weapon Systems

Operation *Allied Force* showed that, after thirty years since their first strike over *Vietnam*, precision weapons had become the weapon of choice in the Air War over *Kosovo*. The weapons used in bombing campaigns have changed from free falling bombs in *WWII* to smart weapons used in *Desert Storm* and *Allied Force* campaigns. These high-tech guided bombs were used nearly 100% against the *Serbian* forces, according to Pentagon sources. A government military analyst said that:…*"one reason is that smart weapons are stand-off weapons released far from the target, thus preventing casualties due to antiaircraft fire and missile defense systems"*…

These weapon systems are very accurate; however, the missile or bomb can mistakenly acquire a nearby target that was not intended to. For example, the bombing of a *Serbian* apartment complex and the bombing of the Chinese Embassy in *Belgrade*.

According to *Kenneth H. Bacon*, chief Pentagon spokesman, smart weapons have completely changed the nature of warfare. As a comparison, during *Operation Desert Storm*, in spite of the dramatic videos shown on CNN, only 9% of the bombs dropped on *Iraq* were smart weapons. By 1995 NATO, during air campaign against *Serbs of Bosnia Herzegovina*, about 70% of the bombs dropped were guided bombs.

John Pike, a military analyst at the Federation of American Scientists, an arms control advocacy group in *Washington* said that:

…"This time we're fighting the war that people thought we were fighting nine years ago"…

meaning Desert Storm. The capability of such weapons was demonstrated during the bombing of the Yugoslavian Army barracks in which the building was flattened completely while the surroundings, in this case a hospital a block away, were practically untouched.

The current U.S. inventory of smart weapons has a major drawback. Most cannot be launched in bad weather. The only exception is the Tomahawk phase III and phase IV, which can operate in all weather. In total smart weapons, about 60,000 of them, are laser-guided bombs. They are identical to conventional iron bombs, except that they have laser seekers on their noses and movable fins for guidance. As demonstrated by airstrikes over Yugoslavia, two airplanes are needed to perform the strike, one to release the weapon and the other to guide it to its target. The bomb automatically adjusts itself as long as the laser remains fixed on target during the attack. However, when weather covers the target, this smart bombs may go awry and off target, thus hitting non-intended targets as the small Serbian coal-mining town of Aleksinance, killing as many as 20 civilians.

…"They are fair-weather friends"…Pike said.

When weather turns for the worse, then NATO forces relied on satellite guided missiles like the $1,000,000 Tomahawk cruise missile launched from submarines or from ships stationed in the Adriatic Sea and from bombers like the B-52.

Another type of munitions currently in use by the U.S. is the so-called JDAMS (Joint Direct Attack Munitions System). In essence, the JDAMS consists of a navigationally equipped dumb bomb guided by signals received from Global Positioning Satellites. All this investment in smart weaponry, during Operation Allied Force, had one objective in mind that was to provide a continuous bombing effort without the need to stop due to weather problems.

The satellite guidance technology is somewhat less expensive than the laser-guided systems. It costs about $50,000 upgrade a dumb bomb with a laser-guided "kit" but only about $18,000 to upgrade with the satellite guidance equipment, according to Pentagon officials.

The Problems

According to Nick Cook, JDW's Aviation Editor London, as NATO embarked on an assault against Serbian ground forces, Nick Cook considered the problems experienced in the allied air campaign. Less than a week into the air campaign launched against Serbia on 24 March, NATO air forces switched to phase II of the operation, striking Serbian ground forces employed in offensive actions in Kosovo.

Despite the relative success of the initial phase, it was directed mainly at the destruction of the Yugoslav military's air defense and command control infrastructure, in essence classic strategic bombing. But few NATO commanders were under the impression of the difficult challenges, or the grave potential risks, that characterized the second and subsequent phases of Operation Allied Force. The air war did not resemble other recent military air campaigns; most notably those mounted against Iraq. The weather in the Balkans was an important factor in hampering operations to precisely locate and track mobile Serb forces and prevented accurate delivery of laser-guided bombs or guided bomb units (GBUs). Based on Nick Cook's report, the UK Royal Air Force's Harrier GR7 strike force had on several occasions aborted missions because of clouds or battle smoke over the target area. RAF sources said they had already noted the problem in Iraq during and after the launch of Operation "Dessert Fox" against Baghdad on December 1998. In attacks on Iraqi air defense sites, a number of RAF GBUs had gone astray because smoke has blocked laser energy between the designator and the target, making the bomb "go astride".

…*"You need good clean air to get a signal"*…
said Lt. Colonel Pierswood of the Washington based Center for Defense Information.

If one adds the problem of battle-smoke to the kind of consistently bad weather experienced during Allied Force, this pointed to a serious shortfall in capability. Based on information obtained from the Center for Defense Information, Lt.Colonel Piers Wood said that:…"highly accurate weapons cannot handle degraded visibility"…

In an interview with Newsweek magazine, Wood commented on weather and obscuration problems as being responsible for affecting the intense highly-focused laser beams needed to lock onto their targets. The problem in this case was more serious than it was seemed, particularly for a campaign anxious to minimize civilian casualties by politically selecting military targets. Air Force commanders found out during previous operations like Dessert Fox, against Iraq that smoke and dust storms could result in rogue bombs that might land miles off target. Colonel Wood also expressed that:

"Precision-guided munitions are like computers,…they tend to be right on the money or way the heck off…if the error (is) electronic, then it tends to be grotesque."

This problem expedited the deployment throughout NATO of fully autonomous weapons systems, such as the US Joint Direct Attack Munition (JDAM). Based on information from USAF officials, irrespective of smoke or cloud conditions, JDAMS, (a strap-on guidance kit for ordinary iron bombs), directed by the satellite-based Global Positioning System (GPS) can hit a target within 13 meters of the pre-programmed target. The first slated aircraft to receive JDAM are the B-1, B-2, and B-52 bombers, the F-16 and the F/A-18 multirole fighters. Of these, only the B-1 and the B-2 were officially cleared for operations. According to Pentagon sources, 3,000 JDAM kits have been ordered, it is thought far fewer have been produced.

In the case of the B-2A Spirit stealth bomber, which had been used in anger for the first time in the campaign against Belgrade, the missdistance for each of its 16 JDAMs can be halved to around 6 meters through the use of the bomber's GPS-Aided Targeting System. Again, poor weather conditions placed even greater reliance than normal on cruise missiles. Actually, both the AGM-86C Conventional Air-Launched Cruise Missiles (CALCM) dropped from B-52s and its sea-launched counterpart, the

Block III version of the Tomahawk Land-Attack Missile (TLAM) relied on GPS guidance for navigation and terminal homing. Cruise missiles targeted particularly air defense centers in the main Serb SAM (surface-air-missiles) chain and at command and control centers. There were also unconfirmed reports that a new variant cruise missile has been used against Serbian electronic and communication centers that uses a conventional blast to simulate the crippling electromagnetic pulse (EMP) of a nuclear detonation. EMP destroys circuitry used in electronic equipment.

Based on interviews conducted from USAF officials, there was a consensus on that no-one in NATO underestimated the ability of Serbian commanders to conceal their air-defense assets in the mountainous and wooded terrain that characterized much of the region. NATO relied on a so called multi-layered reconnaissance architecture in the battle to pin point key Serbian weaponry such as its medium range S-75 Dvina (SA-2 "Guideline"), Perchora-M (SA-3s "Coa") and 2K12 Kvadrat (SA-6 "Gainful") SAM batteries And armour and artillery concentrations in Kosovo. This array of weapons extended from radar-imaging and Electro-optical imaging spacecraft all the way down to unmanned aerial vehicles (UAVs). It was believed that at least some of the radar-imaging assets were capable of penetrating foliage in the hunt for Serbian heavier weapon systems.

NATO officials reported that by the 3rd week in March, Serbian forces appeared to have held back from firing large numbers of their medium SAMs fearing that all their air-defense sites could have been located and picked off in the first wave of NATO attacks. The destruction of a USAF F-117A Stealth Fighter on March 27 pointed to the deployment in Yugoslavia of the Czech-developed TAMARA passive aircraft location device, which was said to be effective against stealth aircraft. U.S. sources believed that the system, which the Czechs have sold to Russia, might have been used in Yugoslavia. According to Jane's Defence Weekly, 1999, TAMARA finds aircraft by homing on signals (radar, radio and even Identification, Friend or Foe emissions), transmitted by the aircraft. It is believed that for an F-117 to be shot down, the aircraft would have had to be emitting some radio signal that otherwise would not do. Also, may be flying the same ingress routes night after night as suggested by Retired Brigadier General McCarthy. NATO was cautious declaring which reconnaissance assets were deployed in the Balkan theatre of operations, but the list was known to be extensive. RAF Nimrod R and US EP-3 and RC-135 Rivet Joint electronic surveillance aircraft were in the forefront of NATO missions to monitor Serbian signals and electronic activity, according to NATO officials. On the imaging side, the alliance relied extensively on the RAF Canberra PR9 long range photo reconnaissance aircraft. Also, the USAF U-2 (a number of U-2 variants were in the theatre, including, it was believed, the ASARS 2 synthetic-aperture radar model) and the US E-8 Joint Surveillance Target Attack Radar System (Joint STARS). The latter, which was used in its early stages, possibly a prototype, during the 1990-1991 Gulf War, provided some effectiveness given the limits of the terrain in plotting Serbian armour movements in real time in Kosovo. It was backed up, according to US military sources, by the Predator long-range UAV and will soon be joined by the U.S. Army's Hunter tactical UAV. In Kosovo, Serbian forces were able and successful in relocating weapons quickly to hamper NATO efforts to destroy them. This was a well-known tactic used by Bosnian-Serbian forces during the mid-nineties and subsequently refined by the Yugoslavians. The alliance's massive reconnaissance effort could have been useless without the ability to pass on attack co-ordinates for these weapons quickly once they have been located.

Battlefield Information

Since the 1991 Gulf War, a considerable effort was undertaken by the United States and its European Allies to convey time-critical intelligence on key enemy mobile weapon systems so that ground attack aircraft can destroy them before they move out of the target area. Based on information obtained from Jane's Defence Weekly, latest variants of the F-16, probably a C, have undergone a range of improvements since 1991 that enable them to exploit this rapid targeting information, as well as to fight and survive more effectively over the battlefield. The end result was a ground attack force able to respond quickly and with precision to rolling intelligence on moving targets around the clock.

According to USAF officials, during the Gulf War, a limited number of F-16s were actually equipped with the LANTIRIN navigation pod and nolaser-targeting pods were available. By the end of the Kosovo campaign, more than 500 LANTIRN systems were delivered for the F-15E Strike Eagle and F-16C/D, with F-16s comprising more than 50% of the USAF's night-precision strike force. In addition significant number of F-16s have also been made compatible with night vision goggle (NVG) equipment, which aids the pilot's situational awareness and complements the use of LANTIRN.

Jane's Defence Weekly reports that, in 1997; these modifications were set in motion on USAF F-16C/D aircraft at Aviano Air Force Base, Italy. By March 1999, this capability was available for front line missions against Serbian forces as part of the USAF's Quick Response Capability (QRC) program. QRC was about rapidly modifying aircraft with the latest technologies in the Balkan theatre of operations. Another F-16 QRC program, "Sure Strike", allowed ground based forward air controllers (FACs) to transmit digital co-ordinates of tanks and other targets directly to an F-16 pilot.

According to USAF official sources, it is believed that Special Forces FACs were sure to have been deployed in Kosovo and perhaps also in Serbia. By April 1994, a unit of UK Special Air Service troops provided vital FAC information from the besieged Muslim town of Gorazde against attacking Bosnian-Serbian forces. The basic ability to transmit targeting data rapidly from intelligence-gathering aircraft such as Joint

STARS via the Improved Data Modem, now equipping the F-16, the A-10 Thunderbolt II tank buster and other combat aircraft had a major impact on the aircraft's ability to effectively operate in the battlefield air interdiction/close air-support (BAI/CAS) role.

Operation Allied Force posed another question on the ability of these BAI/CAS aircraft to survive in the course of prolonged operation to clear Serbian forces from Kosovo. USAF officials believed that during the Bosnian campaign, allied aircraft were reasonably protected against the threat from SA-2, SA-3 and SA-6 SAMs because intelligence on their whereabouts was adequate and because onboard electronic counter-measures (ECM) systems were deemed to offer reasonable protection against radar-guided missiles. However, what seemed impossible to track during the Balkans campaigns were the shoulder-launched infrared (IR) guided missiles. According to Jane's Defence Weekly, in April 1994, an UK Royal Navy Sea Harrier FRS1 was shot down by an Igla-1 (SA-16 "Gimlet") shoulder launched SAM during a NATO mission to destroy Bosnian-Serbian armour outside Gorazde. Therefore, NATO's reaction was to limit the deck for BAI/CAS operations to 10,000 ft, well outside the effective envelope of the SA-16 and weapons like it. But, by doing so, the effectiveness of the attacks decreased significantly. The major problem in operation Allied Force over Kosovo, was compounded by the fact that few NATO aircraft types had adequate missile approach warning systems (MAW) against IR-guided weapons. Without this system to warn or trigger a decoy, a pilot had no choice but to indiscriminately fire off flares at arbitrary intervals hoping to deflect any IR-guided SAMs that were launched. USAF officials said that, the MAW procurement across NATO's fighter fleet was bound to accelerate as a result of the Kosovo crisis.

NATO officials said that, if enough of the munitions systems could have been available for use in Kosovo, NATO's weapon of choice against Serbian armour concentrations would had been the US CBU-97 Senso-Fuzed Weapon (SFW), which has just been cleared for operational use on the B-1B, F-16 and A-10. SFW dispenses submunitions over a target area to seek out and destroy individual armoured targets.

Its main advantage was its capability to be released outside the hand-held SAM and AAA envelope. A recent upgrade to the existing cluster-bomb family, the Wind-Corrected Munitions Dispenser, adds an inertial unit to compensate for wind-drift during the long time of flight from medium altitude release.

Weapons like these greatly assisted NATO in its bid to halt Serbian operations in Kosovo and at the same time limit the serious potential for casualties among NATO aircrews. Without them the results of the Air Campaign would have been different.

Tomahawk Cruise Missile

This long-range, subsonic cruise missile was the weapon of choice when weather conditions did not allow aircraft to fly for land attack warfare over Kosovo, usually launched from surface ships and submarines. This sleek cruise missile was designed to fly at low altitudes and high subsonic speeds and to penetrate tough air defenses.

The missile is piloted over an evasive route by several mission tailored guidance systems. The first successes of the Tomahawk cruise missile were demonstrated during operation Desert Storm in 1991 with immense success. The missile has been since successfully used in several other conflicts. In 1995, the governments of the U.S. and UK signed a Foreign Military Sales Agreement for the acquisition of 65 missiles, making the first sale of Tomahawks to a foreign country. After November 1998 launch and live warhead testing completed, the UK declared operational capability.

One of the features of the Tomahawk Block II is that it uses a Terrain Countour Matching (TERCOM) and Digital Scene Matching Area Correlation (DSMAC) missile guidance system. The newer Block III adds Global Positioning Satellite Guidance capability to TERCOM and

DSMAC. Basically, radar detection of the missile is extremely difficult because of the small radar cross-area section and low flying altitude.

The Tomahawk has two warhead configurations, a 1,000-lb blast/fragmentary unitary warhead and a general-purpose submunition dispenser with combined effect bomblets.

Because of its long range, lethality and extreme accuracy, the Tomahawk has become the weapon of choice for NATO's operation Allied Force.

Currently, the U.S. Navy is operating Block III and Block IV models of the Tomahawk, which are advanced versions of the original missile. Also, the Navy is in the process of developing an even more advanced version known as the "Tactical Tomahawk". The capabilities of the future tomahawk Block IV or "Tactical Tomahawk", according to the Navy, will include battle damage assessment, in flight retargeting, and mission planning from the launch platform. With added technical capabilities, the Tactical Tomahawk will carry on the superior tradition of its predecessor into the 21st century. It is projected to enter service in 2003.

The Air Force currently operates the Conventional Air Launched Missile (CALM) a conventional version of the original Nuclear Air Launched Missile (NALM), which also uses a GPS navigational system. Unlike the Navy, the Air Force did not develop a conventional cruise missile, focusing instead on those capable of delivering nuclear weapons. Given the very different nature of the nuclear mission the Air Force's requirement for cruise missiles was relatively low. The Air Force is currently in the process of converting its cruise missiles for conventional use, but had only an estimated 150 available when air operations began in Kosovo.

The Navy recognized the potential of conventional cruise missiles early during their development, particularly in attacking other ships, and currently has an estimated 3,500 Tomahawks of all types in their arsenal. Since the Gulf War in 1991, however, 95% of all cruise missiles used by the Navy have been Block III or IV, and it is the supply of these particular missiles that were causing concerns during operation Allied Force. In the 1990s the Navy decided that is would halt new production of Block III, preferring to save money by upgrading older models units until the Tactical Tomahawk went into production in 2003.

As part of their planned modernization program, the Navy is requesting $50.9 million in Fiscal Year 2000 for the upgrade of 148 missiles to Block III, and a further $59.6 million in FY01 to upgrade 176 missiles, according to Navy sources. In addition, as reported in Jane's Defence Weekly, the Navy is seeking $113 million in supplemental funds in the current fiscal year for upgrades to 324 missiles, to replace those used during December 1998 in operation "Desert Fox" against Iraq. The Navy has also included funds in the FY00 budget to push up the production date of the Tactical Tomahawk to 2002.

According to press reports, the Air Force, in April 1999, received permission from the Office of Management and Budget to request funding for the conversion of an additional 92 nuclear ALCMs to conventional weapons. The estimated cost is $51 million, which will require congressional approval.

As the air war over Kosovo entered its second week, the U.S. forces were faced with the possibility to run-out of cruise missiles, thus jeopardizing the sustained protracted heavy air operation. Chris Hellman, Senior Research Analyst for Weekly Defense Monitor wrote on 9/28/99 that:

> ..."*from an operational standpoint in Kosovo, the shrinking supply of cruise missiles was unlikely to limit planned strikes...the current arsenal appears sufficient to support continued operations*"...

But, after weeks of sustained air campaign the targets switched from large fixed targets like bunkers, buildings and military bases and communications infrastructure to smaller usually mobile targets like tanks and infantry units. Obviously, a cruise missile was not designed to hit a tank; thus the cruise missile became less effective. During the air campaign, the Navy still had about 1,000 Tomahawks, albeit less capable ones, in their inventory according to Chris Hellman.

At the end of the war, the U.S. forces did not run out of missiles, but there was one indisputable fact, future military campaigns around the world are likely to emphasize the limited supply of top of the line cruise missiles, unless production matches its demand.

Jamming Support

Operation Allied Force showed among other things an area of concern as to the role of stealth technology and jamming support aircraft. In essence stealth technology did not really provide the much-expected reduction in support aircraft needed for combat operations. The air forces optimistic belief in stealth technology was shaken when on March 27, 1999 an USAF F-117A "stealth fighter" was shot down over Kosovo. Immediately, the Air Force started flying F-117As, B-2s and F-22 fighters with jamming support from the Navy EA-6B radar jamming aircraft.

Why the Navy? Because the Air Force decided to retire its fleet of radar-jamming EF-111 "Raven" after a questionable performance in the Persian Gulf War in 1991. The rationale behind the retirement of the "Raven", is that the USAF envisioned a fleet of stealthy F-117As, B-2s and F-22 fighters operating "basically without jamming protection" from conventional aircraft. But the March 27 incident changed all that. The Pentagon, according to Chris Hellman, Senior Research Analyst for Weekly Defence Monitor, needed more radar jamming planes from the Navy, thus overburdening its existing fleet of 91 EA-6Bs "Prowlers", 30 of which were already in use supporting air operations in Kosovo. The new mission for the EA-6B to escort F-117As and B-2s forced the Navy to request at least 50 additional jamming aircraft.

Major General Dennis G. Haines, Air Combat Command's director of combat operations, acknowledged the significance of the Air Force's lack of a jamming capability. At a conference on June 24, 1999, the General said:

> ..."*stealth reduces the signature of an aircraft, but it does not make it invisible. We have really neglected electronic warfare*"...

The EA-6B "Prowler" primary mission is to support strike aircraft and ground troops by interrupting enemy electronic activity and obtaining tactical electronic intelligence within a combat area. The Prowler is a twin engine, mid-wing aircraft manufactured by Northrop Grumman Aerospace Corporation as a modification of the basic A-6 Intruder airplane. Designed for carrier and advanced base operations, the Prowler is a fully integrated electronic warfare system combining long-range, all weather capabilities with advanced electronic countermeasures. Forward equipment bays, and pod-shaped fairing on the vertical fin, house the additional avionics equipment. The side by side cockpit arrangement gives maximum efficient visibility and comfort.

RQ-1A "Predator" UAV

The Predator system was designed in response to a Department of Defense requirement to provide persistent intelligence, surveillance and reconnaissance information to the strike fighters. It was the first successful Advanced Concept Technology Demonstration. This is a new acquisition process designed to reduce costs and development time by relying on Commercial Off The Shelf Technology (GOTS) to the maximum extent possible. In April 1996, the Secretary of Defense elected the USAF as the operating service for the RQ-1A Predator system. The 11th and 15th Reconnaissance Squadrons Indian Springs Air Force Auxiliary Field, Nevada, currently operate the RQ-1A system. Improvement programs currently under development include an ARC210 radio, an APX-100 IFF/SIF with Mode 4, and an ice mitigation system which includes an uprated turbo-charge engine. The Air Force has 3 partial RQ-1A systems, the training systems at Indian Springs AFAF, the deployed system in

TASZAR Air Base, Hungary, and a pre-delivery system undergoing validation and verification. Initial operational capability is planned for October 1, 1999.

The RQ-1A Predator mission is to fly at medium altitude, long range endurance and without a pilot. It is a Joint Forces Air Component Commander owned theatre asset for reconnaissance, surveillance, and target acquisition in support of the Joint Force Commander. The Predator is designed to be employed in moderate risk areas, minimizing the risk to human life. For example, areas where the enemy air defenses have not been fully suppressed open ocean environment, and biological or chemical contaminated environment. The RQ-1A Predator is a system, not just an aircraft. This is a new paradigm for the Air Force. A fully operational system consists of four air vehicles (with sensors), a ground control station (GCS), a TROJAN SPIRIT II SATCOM communication suite, and 55 personnel. The "R" is the Department of Defense designation for reconnaissance; "Q" means unmanned aircraft system. The "1" refers to it being the first of a series of purpose-built unmanned reconnaissance aircraft systems. The "A" says it is the first version of the RQ-1 system series.

The Predator air vehicle and sensors are commanded and controlled by its GCS via C-band line of sight data link or a Ku-band satellite data link for beyond line of sight operations. During flight operations the crew complement in the GCS is an Air Vehicle Operator and three Sensor Operators. The aircraft is equipped with color nose camera (generally used by the AVO for flight control), a day variable aperture TV camera, a variable aperture infrared camera (for low light/night), and a synthetic aperture radar (SAR) for looking through smoke, clouds or haze. The cameras produce full motion video and the SAR still frame radar images. The three sensors are carried on the same airframe but cannot be operated simultaneously.

Each Predator air vehicle can be disassemble into six main components and loaded into a container nicknamed "the coffin". This enables all system components and support equipment to be rapidly deployed worldwide. The largest component is the GCS and it is designed to be rolled into a C-130. The air transportable TROJAN SPIRIT II consists of two Humvees, a 6.1 meter satellite dish, a 2.4 meter dish, and associated support equipment. It provides communications between the ground station and the aircraft when it is beyond line of sight and is a link into secondary intelligence dissemination networks. The RQ-1A system needs 5000 ft x 125 ft of hard surface runway with clear line of sight to each end from the GCS to the air vehicles. All components must be co-located on the same airfield. Pilots who fly the aircraft are all rated pilots who flew C-141 Starlifters, KC-135 tankers, B-52 bombers, U-2s or AWACS aircraft. The pilots flying the Predator remotely use controls found in normal cockpit.

One problem the controllers mentioned was the limited field of view.

During the Kosovo air campaign, Predators collected intelligence, searched for targets and kept cameras aimed at Kosovar-Albanian refugees. The aircraft helped planners assess battle damage and sort out the chaos of the battlefield.

According to Jim Garamone, American Forces Press Service, and the UAV was effective flying over areas deemed too hot for manned aircraft. The almost constant surveillance provided by the aircraft forced Serbian forces into hiding. If the Serbs moved from their positions, they were spotted and reported. If regular acquisition processes had been followed, this battlefield star would have been nowhere near Kosovo. But, thanks to the advanced concept technology demonstration program, it did fly over Yugoslavia.

Based on information reported by the American Forces Press Service, Allied Force was not the first time the Predator, also known as the Medium Altitude Endurance Unmanned Aerial Vehicle has been deployed. The aircraft aided U.S. forces entering Bosnia even before it had finished the demonstration phase. This process allowed the Predator to be deployed to the Balkans in less than 19 months after the program started in 1996. Normally, a new system takes 11 years to reach the field.

The advanced concept technology demonstration allows researchers to find and exploit technologies to solve important military problems. Department of Defense officials will use the information they gained from the Predator to build the next generation of UAVs. The possibility for fighter and bomber roles is also being explored.

Air Force Lt. Col. Mary Meyer, a military assistant with DOD's Advanced Technology Office said:

>…"we need to continue to take and hold the high ground"…

Next up is the $10 million jet-powered Global Hawk. Made by Teledyne Ryan, Global Hawk will be bigger and fly higher and faster than the Predator. Global Hawk will fly for 40 hours and will have a 3,000-mile range and 65,000-ft. ceiling. In a July 6, 1999 memo, Defense Secretary William S. Cohen said that:

>…"the DOD must aggressively push the requirements and acquisition process for Global Hawk…we are at a critical juncture in airborne reconnaissance"…

Also, Cohen wrote in a memo to the department:

>…"forty years ago we were at a similar crossroads and committed to the development of our nation's successful high-altitude manned aircraft…Technology…has moved forward at an amazing pace, and…the demand for information has increased even more quickly…the opportunity is here to develop, acquire and integrate unmanned airborne reconnaissance capabilities into the force structure at a rapid, but prudent rate"…

Joint Direct Attack Munition (JDAM)

This particular weapon system produced by Boeing Company, is a low cost guidance systems kit, which converts existing unguided free-fall bombs into accurately guided "smart" weapons. According to Boeing Company news release information, JDAM includes a new tail section containing an Inertial Navigation System (INS)/Global Positioning System (GPS) guidance to existing inventories of Mk-83 and BLU-110 1,000 lbs. (450 kg) bombs, and the Mk-84 and BLU 109 2,000 lbs. (900 kg) bombs. Boeing Company reported that the cost effective JDAM provides highly accurate weapon delivery in any "flyable" weather. JDAM can be dropped up to 15 miles from a target with updates from GPS satellites to help guide the bomb to the target.

Boeing Company reported that JDAM is nearing completion of the Engineering, Manufacturing and Development (EMD) phase and production contracts for 3139 kits have been signed. Boeing has built 800 EMD and production JDAMs to date. During the EMD, JDAMs were built using production processes, facilities, and people to validate manufacturing processes, support EMD testing, and to produce early operational assets. Boeing Company sated that the initial operational testing was completed on the B-1 and B-2 aircraft and JDAMs were delivered to the B-2 wing at Whiteman AFB, Missouri and the B-1 wing at Elsworth AFB, South Dakota in 1998.

The JDAM production team includes Honeywell Inc. (inertial measurement unit), Rockwell Collins (global positioning system receiver), HR Textron (tail actuator subsystem), Lockheed Martin Tactical Defense Systems (mission computer), and Lockley (tail fairing), Enser and Eagle-Picher (battery), and Modular Devices Inc. and Lambda (power supply). Boeing reported that the team achieved a dramatic record of successes in over 245 guided launches from the B-1B, B-2, B-52, F/A-18 and F-16 aircraft since October 1996. JDAM recorded an unprecedented 95% system reliability while a 9.6-meter CEP accuracy against a 13-meter CEP (including target location error) accuracy requirement. JDAM performance was demonstrated in operationally representative tests including drops through clouds, rain, and snow. These tests included a spectacular display of B-2/JDAM conventional firepower in the release of 16 JDAM from a B-2 on a single pass against multiple targets in 2 target areas, according to Boeing data.

Boeing Company scheduled JDAM production rate is expected to exceed 1000 kits per month. The Department of Defense plans to buy 87,496 JDAMs for use by the Air Force, Navy and Marines under the production program that is expected to continue for over a decade. Licenses for export, according to Boeing, were approved and significant additional sales of JDAMs are expected in the international market.

Boeing Company expected growth of the JDAM family of weapons with the funded Mk-82 500 lbs. Version, followed by 2,000 lbs., which began flight testing in early 1999. Additional growth to the JDAM low cost family of weapons potentially included extending the range to greater than 35 miles, improved GPS accuracy, low cost terminal guidance and additional warheads.

In July 26, 1999, The U.S. Air Force and Boeing Company successfully launched the first Boeing-developed Joint Direct Attack Munition kit for a Mk82 500-lbs. bomb at Eglin Air Force Base, Florida. Carl Avila, Boeing JDAM program manager said:

> ..."the results of the flight are very impressive"..."this was a major milestone As it confirms the Mk-82 as a member of the JDAM family of weapons"...

This first guided launch of the smaller bomb kit impacted within three meters of the target. The accuracy demonstrated was well within the U.S. Defense Department's requirement for the JDAM system. The flight also demonstrated the combined all-weather accuracy of the JDAM and the F-15E radar targeting, according to Boeing.

Chapter II
Bomber Operations

When five B1-B bombers were ordered to deploy to Europe in support of NATO operations in Yugoslavia, in March 29, 1999, it marked a milestone in modern bomber history, according to information obtained from Air Combat Command News Service, Langley Air Force Base, *Virginia*. Operation *Allied Force* was the first time the Air Force's heavy bomber fleet, the B-2 *Spirit*, B-52 *Stratofortress* and B1-B *Lancer* were used together operationally, according to Major J.C. Valle, deputy chief of Air Combat Command's Weapons and Tactics Branch. Lt. Gen. Tom Keck, ACC vice commander put it like this:

> ..."*This major milestone for the bomber force, shows the pride and professionalism of the entire Air Combat Command team*"..."*we are also proving that the Air Force is ready and continues to employ the Expeditionary Aerospace Force concept*".

Also, General Dick Hawley, Air Combat Command commander expressed his views as:

> ..."*I think the great thing that we've seen over the past few years is that all the theatre commanders have begun to recognize the contribution that bombers can make to their operational plans*".

The operation in *Kosovo* validated the Air Force's bomber concept operations as the Air Force's main provider of combat air forces stated above.

According to ACC news service, the ACC provided its heavy bomber fleet of aircraft, B-2s, B1-Bs and B-52Hs to NATO *Operation Allied Force*. Lt. General Tom Keck, vice commander of ACC added to his comments that the Air Force is combining intelligence, surveillance and reconnaissance assets with bomber and fighter strike packages to become an unbeatable force. These sustainable air power packages are "effects driven" and gave theatre commanders what they need when and where they need it. ACC's bomber concept of operations includes using the B-52 initially as a stand-off platform using munitions such as the conventional Air Launched Cruise Missile (ALCM) to begin attacking critical enemy nodes, such as command and control centers early in the fight. General Hawley said that:

> …"we brought the B-52 in early using CALCM. We brought the B-2 in as quickly as we could and started to take out some of those heavily-defended targets deep in enemy territory that no other system can get to, either because other systems can't penetrate or don't have the lethality required. Then, of course, the B-1 got in and they've been doing great work using their ability to drop tons of ordnance, including very effective cluster munitions, to take down important targets in the theatre…so, it is a great validation of our current concept op operation".

The B-1B, with its ability to be packed with other types of aircraft, fighters and other self-protection assets, was used accurately to deliver massive quantities of munitions, according to General Hawley. Actually the B1-B bombers were ordered to deploy to

Europe in support of NATO operations in Yugoslavia in March 29, 1999.

The B-2, with its stealth characteristics, was used to get in and take out high-value targets deep in enemy territory that couldn't be readily destroyed by any other system. The B-2s made their operational debut on March 24 when two *Spirits* dropped 32 2,000-lb. JDAMs (Joint

Direct Attack Munitions) during a 31-hour, non-stop mission from Whiteman AFB, Mo. Brigadier General Leroy Barnidge, 509th Bomb Wing Commander said:

>...*"the jets performed perfectly and the crews performed*
>*even better".*

The B-2's low observable or "stealth" characteristics gave it the unique ability to penetrate an enemy's most sophisticated defenses and threaten its most valued and heavily defended targets. During operation *Allied Force* the B-2 was used in a direct attack role employing Global Positioning System Guided Munitions, according to Major J.C. Valle deputy chief of ACC Weapons and tactics Branch.

The B-52, along range heavy bomber that can perform air interdiction, offensive counter-air and maritime operations was used as a standoff missile launcher during the operation, Major Valle said. In all six B-52s from Barksdale AFB, La., were sent to Fairford, Royal Air Force Base, *England* by February 17, 1999 and took part in the first wave of airstrikes in March 24, 1999. Four additional B-52 bombers and about 30 members from the 5th Bomb Wing, Minot AFB, N.D., were ordered to deploy to RAF

Fairford in March 27.

The B-1B was the backbone of the bomber fleet, and provided massive firepower including general-purpose unguided weapons, cluster bomb units and GPS guided weapons. The B-1B carried more weapons than any other weapon system in the USAF, according to Major Valle. However, the B-52 still provided the greatest flexibility on range to payload in the inventory. The B-1B made its operational debut on December 1, 1998 over the skies of *Iraq* during operation *Desert Fox*. While the milestone is important historically, the much more important factor operationally is integrating all three bombers with the other combat Air Forces. Major Valle said:

>...*"Integrating all aspects of combat airpower is the key to*
>*successful bomber employment".*

The B1-B Lancer Case

Staff Sgt. Carole Pfeiffer from the 53rd Wing Public Affairs provide information on the B-1B deployment to *Kosovo*. The 53rd Bomber Wing helped support the bomber as part of *Operation Allied Force*. The bomber wing developed, tested and fielded new software for the B1-B in less time, about 100 hours, than what normally takes a few months to accomplish. The extra effort paid off and the B-1B joint NATO effort by April 1, 1999, less than a week after the call came for their support.

According to Staff Sgt. Carole Pfeiffer, the unit received a call by March 26, 1999 from the Air Combat Command battle staff. The ACC wanted to send the B-1 to assist in the *Kosovo* crisis, but the aircraft needed an updated software package, known as block cycle update, from the 53rd Wing before it could be deployed. The wing immediately began working around the clock to create new defensive mission data software to incorporate with the block cycle update. The new data link allowed the B-1's electronic warfare system to accurately identify and counter enemy radar.

Help came from military and civilian engineers from the 36th Engineering and Test Squadron, which began writing new mission data software that night, and started testing it the following morning. Technical concerns were addressed and quickly solved, and employ-ment guidance was built. The laboratory testing was completed the morning of March 29, 1999 and fielded by that afternoon, and the flight test accomplished on the evening of March 30, 1999. Lt. Colonel Lou Martucci, 36th ETS operations officer said that:

> …"*the new software has increased capabilities that the theatre commanders were interested in, enhanced defensive capabilities well as new weapons capabilities…to meet the dates they wanted, the electronic warfare mission data had to be done very quickly and optimizations made to the defensive systems.*"

To accomplish this monumental task, the unit required the cooperation of numerous players. For example, many units within the 53rd Wing worked with other military units as well as contractors from Boeing, Raytheon and AIL Systems to complete all phases of the test, according to the 53rd Wing News Center. Also, the 36th ETS built and tested the software, and technicians from the 16th Test Squadron assisted with its validation. The 28th Test Squadron coordinated with ACC to resolve communications and navigation radio issues. The 53rd Support Squadron arranged video teleconferencing and worked computer issues, while the 68th Test Support Squadron provided intelligence support. Then, the 53rd Test and Evaluation Group's Detachment 2 flew a B-1B from

Ellsworth Air Force Base, S.D., to Eglin for the flight-test. According to Lt. Colonel Martucci, normally time on Eglin test ranges for flight tests must be planned weeks in advance. However, according to Martucci, the 46th test Wing allowed them to get on the range immediately when they needed.

On another note, Lt. Colonel Gregg Bourke of the 36th ETS integrated systems flight commander said:

> …"The cooperation we got from Ellsworth was outstanding…the 28th Bomb Wing was not only generating airplanes to go, they were helping us work issues so that we could help them".

By March 29, 53rd Wing members were on their way to Ellsworth to brief aircrews and assist with installation of the new software. Lt. Colonel Martucci added that:

> …"Everyone went way above and beyond what anyone ever thought could be accomplish".

The remarkable team effort achieved by the men and women of the 53rd Wing led to the B1-B flight test in less than 100 hours. If one considers that they started from nothing, the job was indeed remarkable. During the final meeting prior to approving the software, it was determined that the unit came up with the absolute best product available given the conditions and time frames. However, according to Lt. Colonel Bourke, time was not a factor in getting the job done. Regardless of the amount of time that they had, Lt. Colonel Bourke said:

…"We kept the needs of our customers, the actual combat aircrews in mind throughout the test, knowing that their lives depend on us. I feel very confident that they're now well prepared to go to battle."

This particular deployment went above and beyond for B-1Bs during the Kosovo campaign, according to Sgt. Carole Pfeiffer, 53rd Wing Public Affairs. Operation *Allied Force* had most military units working at double-time pace. Some of the units were wearing numerous hats, taking on extra assignments and duties in addition to their primary responsibilities. Even small detachments were no exception. Like the number 2 detachment from the 53rd Test and Evaluation Group, at Ellsworth Air Force Base, S.D.

The story is relevant so see the operations of smaller units in support of their Wings. The small detachment, actually a subordinate unit of the 53rd Wing at Eglin Air Force Base, Fla., had 15 members who were currently performing critical additional tasks while carrying on the unit's primary role as the Air Force's operational B-1B test unit.

Based on information provided by the 53rd Wing Public Affaires Office, when the call came in late March for the B-1 bombers to join the NATO team in the *Kosovo* crisis, the detachment was completing the combat certification process for a hardware and software upgrade to the bomber. This upgrade, known as a block cycle upgrade, converted the B-1B from Block C to Block D, adding precision weapons, satellite navigation and defensive improvements to the aircraft. The involvement of the detachment in the NATO effort did not end there. According to ACC, when the 77th Bomb Squadron at Ellsworth, the unit tasked to fly the B-1Bs in Operation *Allied Force*, obviously, needed additional crewmembers who were trained in the upgraded B-1B, thus the detachment sent four of its 12 crewmembers to join them. Although they were operational test pilots and weapons officers, the crew of four became combat mission-ready in record time. It usually takes 60-90 days to do that, a B-1B instructor pilot said.

While some crewmembers continued to fly combat missions for NATO, this particular detachment remaining pilots and weapons officers at Ellsworth, worked seven days a week to train other B-1B crewmembers on the Block D upgrade. Detachment aircrews were also ferrying additional B-1s to Fairford Royal Air Force Base in England, where the bombers were forwarded and deployed to fly the NATO strike missions. At the same time, with their heavy involvement in the NATO effort, the small unit continued to perform operation tests on the B-1B. Lt. Colonel Rich Olsen, then commander of Detachment 2 said:

> …"*I am proud of the important contributions the members of detachment 2 have made to NATO's efforts in Kosovo…the detachment helped establish the design requirements for the upgrade, tested the combat readiness, and are now proving the capabilities of the upgraded B-1 by flying combat sorties over the Balkans*".

The B-2 Stealth Bomber Case

The allied air campaign over *Kosovo* marked a turning point in aerial warfare at the turn of the 21st century. NATO weapons used in the first few days of operation *Allied Force* ranged from unmanned Tomahawk cruise missiles fired from submarines, ships or airplanes to sophisticated B-2 *Stealth* bomber guided by global positioning systems satellite. Like its legendary predecessor, the B-52, the Northrop B-2 *Stealth* bomber attacked from bases in the U.S., flew half way around the world, hit their target with 2,000-lb. Bombs and returned safely to home. These long range missions were pioneered by the late General Curtis E. LeMay during the outbreak of the Cold War during the early 1950's, using the B-36, B-47 and B-52 bombers. Now, the B-2 mission came more than a decade after the $2 billion tailless winged plane first rolled out into public view.

The original idea behind the B-2 was to have a bomber that could penetrate USSR's defenses and unleash its nuclear payload undetected by radar. But now, the Air Force switched to its conventional role dropping conventional/GPS-guided bombs on Serbia and *Kosovo*. The initial non-stop mission over to *Belgrade* was conducted by a pair of B-2s from Whitman AFB carrying up to 16 precision guided weapons attacking "hardened targets", like command centers and air defense systems, according to senior defense officials under utmost reservation. Thus, the B-2 slipping inside *Yugoslavia's* formidable air-defense system, dropped its weapons, escaped unscathed and return home without endangering U.S. and allied pilots. On an interview conducted by Associated Press on Army General Henry H. Shelton, Chairman JCS, the General said that:

> ... *"The air-defense system in Yugoslavia is very capable and it poses a considerable threat".*

Also, in support of the mission, Defense Secretary William S. Cohen, said that:

> ... *"The aircraft performed according to its capabilities."*

The B-2 weapon system is one of the most argued over defense spending since the Reagan administration. Secretary of Defense William J. Cohen said, in his days as senator, that sending a B-2 into battle would be like dispatching "a Rolls Royce" to pick up groceries in a combat zone. The total cost of the fleet of 21 B-2s was expected to be in the neighborhood of $44—$50 billion dollars and employing 40,000 workers in 38 states.

Its public debut was in November 1988, in a much controversial rollout ceremony. Like any new plane, technical problems are not uncommon. But the B-2, the most controversial plane ever built, was the exception in that sense. Technical problems plagued the new bomber. The radar system had difficulty distinguishing between a mountain and a cloud, the radar-absorbent paint chipped off too quickly, the wing skins (for some unexplained reason) developed holes and ejection seats failed to work properly. Thus congressional boosters, including the U.S. Government congressional leaders, presented the expansion of the B-2 program beyond the planned 21-bomber fleet. According to a senior defense official, the B-2 was selected because of its relatively heavy bomb load, up to 16 2,000-lb. bombs, as compared to the F-117 *Stealth Fighter* which carries 2 1,000-lb. bombs. However, the bomber's ability to drop weapons precisely at night and in all weather conditions remains comparable for both aircraft.

The B-2 showed a remarkable advance in using GPS-guided weapons since the Persian Gulf War in 1991. Now, satellite-guidance systems onboard the B-2 can direct Joint Direct Attack Munitions (JDAM) to their targets without any visible contact or laser designator, clearly a major asset in the B-2s successful combat debut over *Kosovo*.

Another issue is with only a pilot and a co-pilot aboard, the B-2 puts fewer crew members at risk than B-52s, which unleashed cruise missiles from, launch sites outside Yugoslavia.

The B-2 can, in fact, be shot down given the right conditions like being seen by enemy ground crews or fighter aircraft. That is why the USAF was reluctant to use the B-2 bomber in *Yugoslavia*. A single plane being shot down, would have been a terrible blow to Air Force morale, considering the cost of 2 bombers being equal to that of a Navy's aircraft carrier. The Air Force was anxious to prove the bomber's potentiality, but very apprehensive and suspicious of the consequences of losing one. Therefore, the USAF was very selective of who flies the plane. The Air Force has 51 B-2 pilots that are picked in a competitive selection process, somewhat like the one used to choose astronauts. According to L.A.Times Staff writer Paul Richter, in his July 8, 1999 column on the B-2, reported that basically, the Air

Force does not want hot-dog fighter jocks piloting its B-2s. It is looking instead for sober fliers in their 30's (much like the selection for the SR-71).

The pilots most important skill is not what they can do with the joy stick, there is little need to manually steer the highly automated B-2, even in combat, USAF pilots said and according to Air Force Brigadier General Barnidge, commander of the 509th Bomber Wing, flying B-2s:

> …"*the mission of the B-2 bomber was to go in after the highest threat and hardened targets…we kick the door in and make it so others can follow.*"

To do this, the Air Force, depends on analytical problem-solvers who can manage and repair the navigation and targeting systems needing good judgement to carry out bombing missions with extraordinary diplomatic sensitivity *(Paul Richter 07-08-99)*.

In post mission interviews with pilots of the 509th bomb wing, they cited judgement, as one of the skills needed to calibrate bomb fuses to destroy the intended targets without causing excessive collateral damage. In bombing, one can set the fuse to detonate bombs several feet above ground, thus causing maximum destruction or delayed detonation in the order of milliseconds to put-off the explosion until the bomb's nose was buried in the ground with minimum collateral damage.

Paul Richter interviewed pilots after the war. In post-war interviews at Whiteman, several B-2 pilots confessed to experiencing great anxiety on their first combat sorties. But more than one said that the missions went so smoothly that they soon seemed easy, even boring. One pilot said that his wife worried not about a potential lucky shot by enemy air defenses what pilots call a *"a golden BB"*, but about how tired he would be at the end of the mission. The pilots who declined to be identified by name for fear Serbs or their sympathizers would harass or hurt them said that, they did not feel at risk after their first encounters…"*I never felt vulnerable,*" one said.

But from their seats far above the conflict, they witnessed the fearsome intensity of the air war. One pilot, a Major with 11 years of flight experience, said that he would always remember a deafening one-hour bombardment near the end of the war. He and his co-pilot counted their own bombs exploding, one after another, in brilliant white flashes that came 50 to 80 seconds after the munitions were dropped. Not far away, B-52 bombers dropped long strips of 500-lb. bombs that illuminated the nighttime sky to near daylight brightness.

…*"it was brutal, "*one pilot said

The capabilities of the B-2 sent a clear and powerful message to Slobodan Milosevic, one pilot said:

…*" if the United States is angry enough, they can go anywhere in the world, you won't even know they're coming to strike you."*

During *Allied Force* campaign, 6 B-2s were used overall, flying a total of 50 missions, which is less than 1% the Air Campaign totals. However, the B-2 dropped 11% of the bombs used in *Yugoslavia*, about 700 in all.

The Air Force did not release, as this writing, a list of B-2 targets, on the contrary, it is known that it was a B-2 that dropped three bombs on the Chinese embassy in Belgrade, killing 3 people including 2 Chinese intelligence officers. Their strike mission shows the B-2 capabilities to attack congested downtown targets in *Belgrade* and stealthy capable enough to avoid tough and sophisticated air defenses. According to Air Force Officials, the B-2 radar evading capabilities were not completely tested in the war. With Serbian radar installations destroyed and the rest covered with jamming E6-Bs *Prowlers* from the Navy, there was not much radar to be worried about.

The general accounting office, the congressional watch dog agency, was by no means silence about the B-2. The office's critical report questioned the durability of the B-2's special radar deflecting skin and argued that the plane needs so much regular attention that in wartime. The reports says that, it cannot be easily moved to forward bases where it would be of greater use, as reported by Paul Richter, Los Angeles Times staff writer, 07/08/99.

Air Force officials, downplayed the GAC's report by saying that:

…"these are the kind of teething problems that are routine with new panes. "

Andrew Krepineritch, who is the executive director of the Center for Strategic and Budgetary Assessments, an impartial defense advisor, praised the B-2's performance in the Balkans, yet some say "the jury is still out" on some of the technical issues. Some issues like the reduction of maintenance needs from 200 hr/flight to 40 hr./flight. In its strategic role, senior military officials, even long-time critics, vouched that the debut of the B-2 in strategic bombing, was in fact a highly attractive asset to military leaders. Basically, to fly from the U.S. to the target and return, when forward U.S bases are not available is an asset. On the other hand, with a 24 hr. turnaround time, the B-2 is able to reach far away targets, fly faster and farther than the *Tomahawk* cruise missile carried aboard submarines and ships. William H. Arkin, an air power expert, said that:

…"really the B-2 eclipsed the era of the cruise missile."

And some military officials, including Air Force Lt. General Michael Short, U.S. Commander in the *Kosovo* campaign, have called the B-2 and its all-weather satellite guided bombing system, the greatest technology success story of Operation *Allied Force*.

It is predicted that America's regional military commanders when once were cautious about using sophisticated systems like the B-2 fearing losing one, and who delayed the B-2s debut for months, now will turn to it regularly.

The Legendary B-52 *Stratofortress*

During operation *Allied Force*, the B-52 provided a large-scale global deterrence of conventional air power. Currently, the B-52 can carry the full spectrum of conventional weapons as standoff platform to be delivered anywhere in the world against enemy targets and defenses with great precision. The B-52 proved without doubt that no other weapon system in the USAF inventory offers the flexibility and versatility of the B-52. Boeing Company is constantly updating the bomber to maintain it as a national defense resource that stands ready to accept new weapons, tactics and missions with continuous capacity for growth. According to Boeing Company data, the Boeing B-52 *Stratofortress*, soon will enter its fifth decade of operational service. As proven in *Kosovo*, the B-52 continues to be an important element of the U.S. Air Force bomber fleet. Because the B-52 has been kept up-to-date with numerous improvements over the years, it is referred to as the bomber that is not getting older, just getting better. No bomber in the U.S. military history has been called upon to remain operational for the length of time expected of the B-52 based on Boeing Company data sources.

The current status of the B-52H, the latest model, is that the bomber is being upgraded maintaining almost the same external appearance of earlier models, however, it is a completely different airplane. Through the 1980's the bomber had increased range, made possible with more powerful Pratt & Whitney TF-33 turbofan engines, more refined electronic defensive and offensive systems and extremely low-altitude capabilities. Boeing has made major modifications to the B-52H since it entered service, and expects to perform additional improvements into the future assuring the bomber will be viable part of the fleet well into the next century.

During the *Kosovo* air campaign, the B-52 was equipped to carry the Short-Range Attack Missile *(SRAM)*, its use not confirmed, and the Air Launched Cruise Missile *(ALCM)*. The SRAM, being a supersonic air-ground missile with nuclear capability, was not used. However, the ALCM was used successfully launched from nearly 5 miles in the sky far from enemy ground fire or SAMs sites.

During the early part of 1999, Boeing delivered an unsolicited proposal to re-engine the 94 remaining Boeing B-52Hs (64 actually in service) to the U.S. Air Force Logistics Center at Tinker Air Force Base, Oklahoma. According to Boeing Sources, delivery of the proposal culminates a year-long feasibility study. In response to government challenges for acquisition reform, the proposal includes some cutting-edge innovations such as the use of engines currently found on commercial jetliners, a long-term lease arrangement in lieu of the more traditional outright purchase of the engines, and the use of commercial rather than military maintenance support. Boeing would replace the bomber's eight TF-33 turbofan jet engines with four RB-211-535 propulsion systems, provided by Allison Engine Company of Indianapolis, Industries.

The RB-211-535 was selected by more than 80 percent of the World's Boeing 757 operators and has been in service for more than a decade. If accepted, the proposal calls for the engines, related-accessory equipment and long-term maintenance support to be provided by Allison. Boeing selected the RB-211 through a competitive analysis of major commercial engine manufacturers. According to Boeing Company, Boeing in Wichita, Kansas will perform management of the re-engine program. In addition to the actual aircraft modifications and engine installations, Boeing also will manage fabrication of necessary hardware at Boeing locations in Tennessee, Texas and Washington. According to Boeing Company reports, in making the proposal, Boeing noted that with the B-52 fleet scheduled to remain in the Air Force inventory for the next quarter century. The lease of commercial, off-the-shelf engines and related equipment will, by conservative estimates, save the Air Force and the American tax payers about $6 billion in operation and support costs over the remaining life of the aircraft, or $200 million a year. Potential value of the proposal to Boeing is about $1.3 billion. Boeing currently is working on a Conventional Mission Upgrade Program that involves transferring the conventional weapon capability from the older, no longer in service, B-52G to the B-52H. The modification provides the capability to accommodate HAVE NAP and *Harpoon* missiles and the universal bomb bay adapter, as well as integrated conventional stores management and global positioning systems for

JDAM (Joint Direct Attack Munitions). Boeing has completed a production program for the Common Strategic Rotary Launcher *(CSRL)*. The units are installed on the B-52H. The CSRL is designed to carry SRAM and ALCM, as well as gravity nuclear weapons.

Chapter III
The Airlift Command

Army/Air Force Logistics

The air war over *Kosovo* showed, among other things, the limited logistic ability of the U.S. Air Force in responding to international conflicts Based on data obtained from Air Force officials, there was a mismatch between the Air Force Air Mobility Command and the Army. Mismatches in this area could cost the U.S., in the near future, precious strategic advantage by not being able to respond in a timely manner, according to George Wilson, veteran defense correspondent. As a consequence, accidents and or casualties could occur if appropriate measures are not taken now.

As of this writing, true facts about the logistics of operation *Allied Force* is still circulating inside the Pentagon, possibly classified. However, one thing is known for certain, that is the Army's post audit on the questionable deployment of the *Apache* helicopter to *Albania*. According to Army sources, it took 31 days for the Army to ship 24 *Apache* helicopters from Germany to *Albania*. Also, the Army bought more M-1 tanks than it can deal with, thus becoming heavier to move. A lot heavier, nearly 50% by the start of the new century according to projections in the air mobility study.

During recent years, the Army was talking about becoming lighter, faster and more responsive, similar to what the British do now. But, the contrary has happened. The *Crusader* artillery rig became a loadmaster's nightmare, adding time to the loading operation and weighing the Army down. If the Army becomes heavier, then, the Air Force lifting capacity will have to increase, either by adding more planes or making bigger ones. In either case, the U.S. Air Force, incase of need, could use its agreement with the airlines to transport troops and leave the Air Mobility Command to move the heavy equipment. According to the Air Mobility Command, the Boeing C-17, the transport of choice, is getting high in the neighborhood of 335 million a piece. According to the Pentagon's latest cost estimate, that includes research and development. The question is can the Air Force afford to buy more C-17s when the money is being used to pay for the F-22 fighter? At this point the answer remains debatable. Is there a LeMay look alike in the Pentagon who can see and understand the logistics problem?

In analyzing the airlift problem, one could acknowledge (unofficially), that a problem exists and the current logistic capabilities are not sufficient. Then, one must look at all other options to move the Army to another continent. According to Army experts, it is nearly impossible to airlift a heavy armored division from the U.S. to distance places like *Middle East* or *Korea* in about 90 days. It could be done, they said, if the time line is stretched. Why not then move the Army's heavy equipment by sea rather than by plane, as stated by George Wilson, veteran defense correspondent.

Operation *Allied Force* showed logistic deficiencies between the Army and the Air Force. Communications between air and ground was one of them. The *Apaches*, by the Army's own admission, arrived in Albania not ready to fight and with a lack of logistic support. In a report written by Brigadier General Dick Cody to Army Chief of Staff, Erik Shinseki, General Cody said:

…"I am convinced that if the Apache crews had not received more night vision training after arriving in Albania, we would have sustained several wire strikes and possibly one or two midair collisions."

Communications run by means of radio and satellite, to organize and coordinate the logistic needed for such a deployment. According to one Pentagon official:

…"the way things are going, we'd have to put enough satellites to black out the sun."

Lack of communication costs time and lives as proven in previous wars. In case of the Apache deployment, lack of night-equipment, experienced pilots and support personnel including lack of night radios, outdated fuel tanks and electronic jamming, showed the absence of a logistic structure in the Army.

Airlift Control Flights

The Headquarters of the Air Force Reserve Command provided information on Airlift Control Flights during the air war over *Kosovo*. Airlift Control Flights provided a cadre of trained personnel to manage, coordinate and control air mobility missions. Part of the Air Mobility Command global command and control structure, these deployable units provided a capability for operating missions at locations where there was limited support. An ALCF can sustain operations under bare base requirements, according to the Air Reserve Command.

Air Reserve Command

Reserve ALCFs deployed as Air Mobility Command's Tanker Airlift Control Elements. A TACLE consisted of a cadre of operations and communications personnel complemented by mission supports elements from various other specialties, such as aerial port, maintenance, weather and security. TALCEs deployment in support of special assignment airlift missions *(SAAMs)*, jointed airborne air transportability training *(JA/ATT)*, training exercises, tanker support, and contingency or emergency relief missions.

Reserve ALCFs own the same sophisticated communications packages and train to the same standards as their active-duty counterparts.

To qualify for ALCF duty, members must have substantial flying or operations planning experience. Like the associate-flying program, ALCF personnel may work deployed mission independently or beside their active-duty counterpart, according to AFRC. Also, six of the 12 AFRCunits were activated in Operations *Dessert Shield* and *Desert Storm* and about the same number in their deployment over Kosovo. Since then, Reserve ALCF personnel have participated in every major deployment involving Air Force strategic airlift forces. Reserve participation by ALCF reservists is high, averaging 130 days of duty annually, based on AFRC.

Airlift Operations

According to data obtained from Headquarters of the Air Force Reserve Command, their airlift mission involves training for transporting people, equipment and supplies to meet U.S. armed forces requirements anywhere in the world. This mission and other roles, including fighter, air refueling, and airborne warning and control system missions, made the Reserve a key element in supporting Operation *Allied Force.*

The Air Force Reserve Command concentrates on the Global Reach or Global Power concept pioneered by General Curtis E. LeMay during the *Cold War.* Reserve aircrews operate unit-equipped aircraft or, through the Reserve's associate program, fly active duty aircraft. Some crews provide long-range, worldwide airlift, and others perform shorter-range transport of troops and cargo.

The 452nd Air Mobility Wing, March Air Reserve Base, California, was the first unit, active or reserve; to receive the C-141C *"glass cockpit"* modified *Starlifter.* The 452nd has undertaken responsibility for operational testing and evaluation and for developing initial cadre aircrew training. The second Reserve wing to receive the C-141C is the 445th Airlift Wing, Wright-Patterson Air Force Base, Ohio. The 433rd Airlift Wing, Kelly Air Force Base, Texas, was the first reserve wing to be assigned the long range, heavy lift C-5A *Galaxy* aircraft. The 459th Airlift Wing, Andrews Air Force Base, Md., was the first reserve unit to own and operate the smaller but still worldwide capable C-141B *Starlifter.* The 439th Airlift Wing, Westover Air Reserve Base, MA., was the second Reserve wing to be equipped with the C-5A; and the 907th Airlift Group (now 445th Airlift Wing), Wright Patterson Air Force Base, OH., was the second Reserve unit to receive the C-141B.

About half of the Reserve's airlift units fly and own the shorter range C-130 *Hercules.* Its speed, range, load carrying characteristics and capability to operate under difficult terrain conditions make it an invaluable and versatile aircraft. It is strong enough to deliver cargo on unimproved landing strips. Other missions involve aeromedical evacuation and special air support operations. More than 9,100 reservists trained in the C-130 airlift mission in a variety of aircrew, aircraft maintenance and support skills. During operation Allied Force, the AFRC provided 20% of the Air Force's C-130 missions.

Although primarily tasked with air refueling other aircraft, the Reserve's KC-135 *Stratotankers* also airlift cargo and personnel. In Air Mobility Command gained associate units, reservists train with active duty units and fly active duty aircraft. Six different types of aircraft are flown to support the associate airlift mission: the C-141 *Starlifter,* C-5 *Galaxy,* C-9 *Nightingale,* C-17 *Globemaster III,* KC-135 *Stratotanker* and KC-10 *Extender.* Because they have dual capability as an aerial refueling or cargo transport, the KC-10 and KC-135 were the backbone of the Air Force's refueling operations over *Kosovo.* Up to date, more than 27,000 members train and support the Reserve's long range airlift missions.

C-17 Operations

The C-17 *Globemaster III* proved its worth in Operation Allied Force, as stated by 1st Lt. Dave Huxsoll, from Aeronautical Systems Center

Public Affairs. Basically, the C-17 accounted for more than 75 percent of the strategic airlift missions over *Kosovo*, while comprising less than 15 percent of Air Mobility Command's strategic airlift fleet.

…"It has become the airlifter of choice,…"

said Colonel Ted Bowlds, director of the C-17 System Program Office. Also, he stated that:

…"Our customers are very satisfied, and commanders are demanding more and more of it."

> *The C-17 SPO is procuring 120 of the new heavy lifters for the Air Force, which has taken delivery of 51 aircraft up to now.*

As of June 29, 1999, C-17s from Charleston Air Force Base, SC., have flown 1,092 missions over *Kosovo*, with a departure reliability rate of 96 percent, according to the Air Force. These include the initial deployment of soldiers and equipment; deployment of *Apache* attack helicopters and their support units to *Albania*; providing supplies to *Kosovo* refugees in *Albania*; deployment of peacekeepers to *Kosovo* and the ongoing re-deployment of forces from allied bases in Europe.

Bowlds commented that three factors accounted for the success of the C-17 in operation Allied Force, and related operations in the Balkans. Those were high payload capacity, ability to land on short, austere airfields and ground maneuverability. Colonel Bowlds also explained that the C-17 could carry four times the payload of a much smaller C-130, yet land in the same area, airfields as short as 3,000 feet and the ability to move in confined areas. Unlike any other large transport aircraft, the *Globemaster III* can back up and turn around, much like an automobile. Also, the C-17 does not have to be reconfigured to off-load different types of cargo. All cargo and equipment can be rolled directly off the aircraft. This means that the C-17s have about three times the "through-put" of similar heavy-lift aircraft. A single C-17 can carry almost three times as many tons per day as other similarly sized transport aircraft. All these features made the C-17 uniquely suited for operating in Albania's Rinas Airport, where the aircraft delivered weapons and equipment for the Army as part of Task Force Hawk, according to Colonel Bowlds. The runway there is small, and taxi and parking areas are extremely limited. C-17s were able to fly in, quickly off-load equipment, and supplies, turn around, and fly out. No other heavy aircraft in the world would be able to do this, said Bowlds.

All C-17 aircraft flying into the area were equipped with protective crew armor, developed by the SPO in less than two weeks, when the Air Force first began operations in Bosnia in December 1995. Colonel Bowlds said that the SPO responded to an increased demand for the armor by increasing its buy of ship sets. Almost all of the Air Force's 51 C-17 were involved in the *Balkan* operation. Military planers were able to use as many of the aircraft as they did, thanks in large part to streamlined management and manufacturing approaches developed by the SPO and Boeing, the aircraft's manufacturer. As of June 1999, 39 C-17s have been delivered consecutively ahead of schedule. As many as 20 C-17 missions were being flown into Albania each day. Colonel Bowlds added:

…"One aircraft was flying operational missions within two days of being delivered to the Air Force."

The aircraft was so much in demand that none was available for display at the Department of Defense Joint Services Open House, held on May 15-16 at Andrews Air Force Base, MD., or the Paris Air Show, held June 13-20. Colonel Bowlds said that the Kosovo crisis not only highlighted the value of the C-17, but also provided an opportunity to make improvements, and added:

…"our challenge is to continue delivering a weapons system in which crews are confident, and that maintains a high mission-capable rate."

Aerial Refueling Operations

The Air Force Reserve Command (AFRC) directly supports worldwide aerial refueling and cargo hauling missions, flying KC-135 Stratotankers (cargo tankers) and KC-10 Extenders (advanced cargo tankers). Reserve squadrons equipped with KC-135 aircraft accomplish about 13 percent of the KC-135 aerial refueling requirements. In associate units, Reserve KC-135 and KC-10 squadrons train with active-duty units and fly active duty aircraft. Associate KC-10 units provide 50 percent of the KC-10 crews and contribute 50 percent to the maintenance force.

The military equivalent of the Boeing 707 transport, KC-135 and KC-135R aircraft can carry 120,000 pounds (54,000 kilograms) of transfer fuel. The KC-135E has an approximate range of 2,562 miles (3,919 kilometers), and the KC-135R has approximately range of 2,800 miles (4,480 kilometers).

The KC-10, similar to its civilian, the McDonnell Douglas DC-10, can carry almost twice as much fuel as the KC-135. It also can carry up to 170,000 pounds (76,500 kilograms) of cargo, three fourth as much as the Air Force's largest cargo plane, the C-5 Galaxy, and twice as much as the C-141 Starlifter.

Operation Allied Force saw the deployment and operation of KC-135s and KC-10s. The total inventory consists of 373 KC-135s active duty and 268 ANG (Air National Guard) and Reserve, of those a total of 250 were deployed over the Balkans. The KC-135 Stratotanker's principal mission was air refueling. This asset greatly enhanced the capabilities of the U.S. Air Force to accomplish its mission of continuous bombing over Yugoslavia. It also provided aerial refueling support to U.S. Navy, U.S. Marine Corp. and allied aircraft. The AMC (Air Mobility Command) manages more than 442 Stratotankers at any given time (primary aircraft assigned), of which the AFR and ANG fly 268 of those in support of AMC's mission.

According to AFRC News Service, as of mid-April, 1999, KC-135 air refueling aircraft and C-130 transport aircraft provided most of the Air Force Reserve Command's support in the Balkans. Eight KC-135 aircraft, 15 aircrews and dozens of support personnel were in Istres, France, to refuel NATO combat aircraft I the region. Another two KC-135s and crews provided air refueling from Geilenkirchen, Germany, during the last two weeks of April 1999. Five C-130s, nine crews and support personnel were deployed to

Ramstein Air Base, Germany. They were there to shuttle Kosovo refugees from the southern Balkans to other areas of Europe and to deliver much needed supplies to other refugees and to NATO forces participating in the operation. Most of the 327 reservists deployed overseas in support of Kosovo were in the aircraft maintenance and other logistics specialties. Other participating career fields included aerial port, medical and communications. Reservists involved in these kinds of missions usually remained overseas for two weeks and were then replaced by other reservists on a rotational basis.

Major Eric Sillery, tanker aircraft operations officer for Headquarters AFRC's directorate of operations said:

…"the number of KC-135s and personnel deployed was about double what was originally planned…that deployment was scheduled to end by July 8, 1999 but it is now open ended. Our people will support the mission for as long as possible."

Major Sillery said that Reserve crews on larger, long-range aircraft, C-5s, C-17s, C-141s and KC-10s were supporting operations in the Balkans on as required bases. Most of the Reserve's strategic aircraft units flew one or more missions in support of the Kososvo operation. Also, Major Sillery said that:

…"the KC-135s were needed to keep the air campaign going…the C-130s were able to land at and take off from small airfields and don't take up as much space as larger aircraft…both kinds of aircraft were ideally suited for this mission."

In an interview with Colonel Holshouser, commander of the 452nd Refueling Wing at March Air Reserve Base, the author inquired about the operational logistics of the tanker squadrons in support of operation Allied Force in the Balkans. In Colonel Holshouser's estimation, a total of 250 tankers including KC-10 Extenders and KC-135 Stratotankers were deployed by the AMC (Air Mobility Command) before the ACC (Air Combat Command), thus creating a support ring around Kosovo. The AMC formed GSUs (geographical support units), each of these units had a *total of 24 KC-135s (8 from France, 16 from Hungary) and another 34 assigned to JTAR including 12 KC-10s.*

In questioning Colonel Holshouser about the AMC's capability in supporting the war effort for another six months, the Colonel replied:

… "absolutely, the AMC had more tankers than needed, had the resources, and the support."

The AMC operated in packs of eighth aircraft that could be ready in 24 hours. AMC depended on aircraft provided by the AFR and ANG. However, aircraft provided by the AFR and ANG were chopped (commands were stripped to form cells) to provide aircraft to the European command. And if one squadron does not has the equipment or personnel to support the European Command, then, the squadron commander was required to ask another squadron to see if they can provide the necessary personnel. This is the so-called "Rainbow" operation allowing squadrons to be combat ready, according to Colonel Holshouser.

Some of the logistical factors that affected tanker operations over Kosovo, according to Colonel Holshouser, were maintenance parts to support 2,100 sorties of which 860 were flown before maintenance was needed. Keeping the supply line open kept the tankers flying. In Colonel Holshouser's opinion, there were some deficiencies on forward bases like Budapest, Rumania. This meant that the airport did not has the minimum maintenance and logistics equipment to support the tankers. These supplies came from USAFE, "E" for Europe, to provide combat support within 24 hours.

In order to cover all NATO attack sorties, the AMC had sufficient tankers to do the job. The AMC provided 100 percent support of combat operations, growing from an initial operational ratio of 50 percent to a full 100 percent, as the air war progressed. However, the air campaign took more of a progressive tone and targets were politically selected, like in Vietnam, Colonel Holshouser said:

… 'is the making of Vietnam all over".

Politically selecting a target hindered the military's ability to do a satis-factory job. Colonel Holshouser expressed that there was no agreement on what to shoot at. Thus, the tankers were ready, on station; no target, no mission and the tankers were sent back to base, dumping fuel in the process to land under the maximum landing weight. In terms of operational effi-ciency it was a waste of resources, wear and tear on aircraft and crews.

Some lessons were learned during operation Allied Force *that could be used to support future AMC operations in international conflicts. Colonel Holshouser explained that chopping tankers from squadrons was not a good idea. For example, a plane from the 452nd Reserve Wing is sent to Europe, once it enters European airspace it no longer belongs to the 452nd wing (operationally speaking). Control of the aircraft is assumed by the European command, thus the AMC no longer supports the aircraft. This is not an efficient way to use logistics. Colonel Holshouser proposed the idea for the AMC to retain control of the assets (KC-135s, KC-10s) thus keeping a constant support to maintain and operate the aircraft. Also, who does own the aircraft? Who is in charge?*

A split command violates the basic management practices, thus creating an on-going problem between the AMC and foreign commands as sup-porting the aircraft is concerned.

During the Kosovo campaign two lines of strategies emerged. General Wesley Clark's, supreme allied air commander, approach was basically to go after mobile targets and destroy them. Lt.General Michael Short's, air com-mander for the Balkans *operation, was more of a traditional strategist and believed in cutting the enemy's supplies infrastructure and command cen-ters. Eventually, General Short won the argument. But, according to Colonel Holshouser, General Short had a fighter pilot mentality believing that a tanker is needed to support a fighter anywhere, without considering how to use assets properly. Colonel Holshouser expressed that the AMC could base a liaison team from AMC recommending how to properly use AMC's assets (tankers) in an AMC-ACC joint operation. Thus, having expertise from the start, preventing communication breakdown, improving joint operations and using logistics support efficiently. Also, according to the author, one should look back at General LeMay's operations during the 1950s when the General had tankers and bombers to deploy the Global Power Concept.*

As far as the pilots were concerned, colonel Holshouser said that there were some days during the campaign in which pilots were finding their jobs easier to do. Eventually, missions became more difficult as the air campaign progressed. There were no differences, no major changes or factors as the operation progressed. The tanker's air operation resembles the civilian Air Traffic Control in the United States. The AMC used tracks flown at level 220, 180, 240 (22,000 ft., 18,000 ft., and 24,000 ft.) in patterns of 1, 6, and 8 airplanes. Sometimes airplanes were vertically separated at 500 ft. The Air Reserve aircrews maintained a ratio (crew/aircraft) of 2 crews per aircraft or 2:1 ratio flying about 10 to 12 hours, resting 8 hours per shift. Air National Guard units flew 14 to 15 hour missions, thus showing some pilot fatigue according to an interview held at March Air Reserve Base with Colonel Richards, commander of the Air National Guard Wing. There was no rotation of aircrews and everybody stayed until the job was done.

The overall feeling, according to Colonel Holshouser, was that pilots found their jobs rewarding and interesting and the pilots were motivated to do their jobs. A good example of this was the rescue by a tanker crew of an A-10 pilot over Bosnia.

Master Sgt. Gregg Bade of the 6th Air Refueling Wing Public Affairs recorded the event. On the of March 27, the fourth night of the air campaign in Kosovo, a KC-135 tanker departed from Moron Air Base, Spain to refuel an RC-135 and a pair of F-16s over the Adriatic. After that, the KC-135 crew received an urgent call from NATO AWACS (Airborne Warning Control Aircraft) controller redirecting the tanker, immediately, to head for Bosnia. According to Bade's report, the crew was given no additional information, but sensed something unusual was going on as they listened to the anxious tone of the AWACS controller's radio calls to other aircraft. Captain Clifton Janney, aircraft commander said:

"We could tell he was task-saturated and very preoccupied…because he didn't give us additional guidance, we proceeded to a pre-established refueling track over Bosnia were we off-loaded fuel to two A-10s and an MC-130. Pretty soon we began hearing conversations between Magic (the call sign for the AWACS controller) and an aircraft with the call sign Sandy 30."

According to Janney's report, the tanker crew could hear Sandy 30 ask the AWACS controller for vectors (compass headings) to the nearest tanker, Sandy 30 needed a tanker immediately. To get to the Sandy 30, *an A-10* Thunderbolt, *the tanker had to descend below minimum altitude for refueling operations in that area, risking being exposed to surface-to-air missiles. At the time of contact with the A-10, the KC-135 off-loaded about 10,000 lb. pounds of fuel to it, considering the A-10 takes only 11,000 lbs. of fuel, the* Thunderbolt *was very close to run out of fuel. Later, the KC-135 returned to its base at Moron, with 17,000 lbs. of fuel, 3,000 lbs. below the minimum 20,000 lbs. required for landing, according to Janney.*

The success of the mission was attributed to proper training in CRM (cockpit resource management), according to Major Kevin Torres, the tanker's navigator. Captain Janney agreed with Major Torres's assessment by saying that:

"it may sound like a cliché to some people when we say we fight the way we train, but it's true, you could have put any Air Force tanker crew in our situation, and the results would have been the same."(www.af.mil/news/jul1999.com)

Chapter IV

Deployment of the Ah-64 Apache

The Apache Case

Why did it take the Army so long to deploy the *Apache* over *Kosovo*? Why were they deployed? There are two basic considerations on this issue. Firstly, the *Apache* helicopter was designed to be tank/artillery busters operating over friendly troops. Without friendly troops below them, they are vulnerable to shoulder fired surface to air missiles. Secondly, as a geopolitical consideration, there was a rumor that the White House gave orders those losses be kept to an absolute minimum. The bombing was executed from 15,000 ft. instead of 5,000 ft. (at 5,000 ft. it is easier to see if the target is real or a decoy). Again, geopolitical factors, like in *Korea, Vietnam, Desert Storm* and now *Kosovo*, forced the U.S. armed forces to fight with one hand tied behind our backs, as stated by Brig. General James R. McCarthy, USAF Ret.

By April 1999, after a week of relentless bombing, the air war over *Kosovo* did not show significant improvement on the ground. Weather provided a safe heaven for *Serbian* troops and high altitude strikes proved inefficient to deter troops on the ground from expelling more ethnic *Albanians* out of *Kosovo*.

In order to boost airpower, the United States announced on April 4, 1999 the deployment of 24 *Apache* helicopters to Albania along with 2,000 supporting troops *(BBC News, April 9, 1999)*.

The twin turbine AH-64 all weather *Apache* is actually the U.S. Army's main attack helicopter. Its offensive armament consists of laser-guided *Hellfire* missiles and M-60 machine guns designed primarily to attack tanks and other armored vehicles forward of friendly troops on the ground. It has a crew of two and its versatility, during day or night, was well proven during *Desert Storm* in January 1991. Initially its deployment created the impression of giving NATO commanders another tool to work against *Serbian* forces in *Kosovo*. But in spite of Pentagon's claims that the Apache deployment was reinforcement to NATO airstrikes, the name "tank busting helicopter" is a synonimum of ground war.

The bad weather over the Balkans significantly reduced NATO's effectiveness in its airstrikes and the Alliance's strategy to prevent further atrocities throughout *Kosovo*. NATO's primary strategic and tactical bombing was against industrial targets, oil storage depots, and bridges, railyards and national command centers. Then the attention turned toward the *Serbian* police and Army units in the heart of *Kosovo* itself. The initial idea behind the *Apache* deployment was to force *Serbian* troops to withdraw or terminate them, should any of them confront the *Apache*, according to Army sources. But the *Balkans* region is a very dangerous environment and is not the open desert of *Iraq*. Serbian troops posed a threat to the Apache pilots without proper ground support.

On April 21, 1999, the first U.S. Task Force equipped with AH-64s *Apache* helicopters received the order to deploy and arrived to Tirana, Albania's capital after a much anticipated wait, for nearly a week, in Aviano's Air Force Base, Italy. The *Apache* task force comprised half of the total of 60 helicopters, including *Black Hawks* and *Chinooks*, that were planned to arrive earlier, but due to lack of logistics and bad weather supposedly delayed their arrival.

The contingency of helicopters, 60 in all, was not entirely equipped with AH-64s, it also had UH-60 *Black Hawks* and CH-47 *Chinooks* from the 12th Aviation Brigade. The *Apaches* belonged to the 11th Aviation Regiment which NATO commanders intended to use against Serbian troops and artillery in *Kosovo,* something the jets, flying at 15,000 ft. could not do. Forty-eight *Apaches,* divided into two squadrons composed the basic structure of the 11th Aviation Regiment, according to Army officials. Both squadrons were deployed, but with a total of 24 *Apaches.* Pentagon's spokesman Air Force Major General Chuck Wald said that by April 17, the deployment of the remaining 24 *Apaches* from the two squadrons had not yet been approved. Why? It is believed that a partial deployment showed signs of political reservations in deploying the Apache and is not indicative of a military command decision.

According to several *Task Force Hawk* sources, the flight of the Apaches from Pisa to Tirana was further divided into four cells, each cell with a combination of CH-47s and UH-60s distanced 90 minutes apart. They all arrived at Tirana on around the evening of April 21. The next flight arrived in Tirana the following day on April 22. The initial orders to the unit were to conduct preparatory planning and mission rehearsal for several days in anticipation to their first combat mission, something the *Apache* never accomplished.

Air Force General Chuck Wald said in Washington, on April 22, 1999 that:

…"so this is additive to the air campaign…at he CINC's decision they'll start employing and they'll be integrated into the air campaign as a signergistic part of the air campaign."

When the first contingency of helicopters arrived in Tirana, it was greeted by a large number of Press officials that waited for a week the much anticipated AH-64 Apache. According to Task Force Hawk officials, there were several factors that contributed to the delay in deploying the helicopters over Kosovo. In a report published by the Army Times on May 3, 1999, Aviation Regiment Commander Colonel Ollie Hunter answered to the question of why the Apache was delayed. The number one reason was force protection, and the number two reason was force protection and number three would be force protection. Colonel Jeff Schoesser, commander of the 12th Aviation Brigade, confirmed on Aril 19 that the helicopter had been ready to deploy for several days. But, according to the Colonel:

…"any force the size of Task Force Hawk has to first and foremost provide for its own security in there, and they have to do that very quickly."

From the military point of view, the above statements are understandable and make logistic sense.

The Logistics

To protect Task Force Hawk, *the ground Army units were comprised by the 1st Armored Division's First Battalion, 6th Infantry Regiment, from Baumholder, Germany and the 82nd Airborne Division's 2nd Battalion, 505th Parachute Infantry Regiment from Fort Bragg, NC. The anti-aircraft protection was provided by elements of the 15th Battalion, 4th Air Defense Artillery Regiment including their Avenger air defense missile system. Actually, this contingency of troops, about 2,000 strong, were deployed before Task Force Hawk left Pisa to give the green light for the arrival of the* Apache.

The U.S. Army troops leading the Apache found the conditions and infrastructure of the airfield in terrible shape. Water, mud and debris from weather conditions posed a challenge for the U.S. soldiers. According to Colonel Shoeder's comments, the challenge for the soldiers was to prepare space to bed down the helicopter. In military language "bed down" means giving the soldiers a place to sleep and eat, a place where they can operate and in their case as place to maintain and arm the aircraft on a daily bases rain or shine. Task Force officers stated that refueling the Apache was difficult task for the Task Force operating in treacherous conditions. Another logistic problem was the coordination of operations with the Air Mobility Command. Cargo planes bringing military equipment for the Task Force were competing for runway and parking space with other transports involved in the Humanitarian mission to relief ethnic Albanians. Also, Task Force officials told that an U.S. based congressional delegation visited on around Apri.l17, unloading necessary aviation equipment out of a C-17 on the airfield tarmac, taking space reserved for the Apaches. A logistic mistake that delayed the AH-64's arrival.

The Morale

The aircrew's morale was high, but with a sense of apprehension. CW2 Goffy Helms, a Black Hawk pilot in Charlie Company, 15th Aviation Regiment, put it succinctly like this:

…"I think we all feel the quicker we get there, the quicker we can help."

Another Black Hawk pilot said CW3 Marces Alberghini:

…"It's time to go do what we get paid for."

Lt.Colonel George Bilafer, commander of the 6th Squadron, 6th Cavalry Regiment one of the two Apache squadrons said:

…"The boys are ready…they are well trained…everybody's head is in the game."

But, were the Apache and its crews really ready as described by Lt. Colonel Bilafer?

On the way to Albania from Pisa, one of the Apaches had to return to the airport due to engine trouble. The rest of the flight continued without incident through the Italian countryside, down the coast for a final refueling spot at Brindisi, a U.S. base maintained for special operations for years. At Brindisi, the Apaches were refueled for the last time before their final leg to Tirana, including loading them with live ammunition for their M-60's and one Hellfire for self-protection, according to Task Force officials. Their flight took them over the Adriatic Sea into the Albanian coastline. They were flying very low and very fast. The assigned airfield came into view presenting a very depressing picture, where flood, mud and water were awaiting them, Allberghini stated:

…"We've got animals crossing the runway…it look like dogs…that's all we needed wild dogs."

The arrival of the Apache was an eye-catching event, one pilot said:

…"welcome to the war…wheels down in Albania, history in the making."

A little after that, Sgt. James Walker of the armament platoon, D Troop, 6-6 Cavalry, reflected on the trip :

…"We sure did have some nice scenery on our way to hell. "

Consequences

On April 26, 1999 and after the initial deployment of the Task Force Hawk, *an AH-64* Apache *attack helicopter crashed landed during a practice manoeuvre somewhere in the Albanian mountains. The exercise was designed in preparation to confront* Serbian *troops in Kosovo. According to a report from Sean D. Naylor, correspondent for Army Times, the aircrew personnel at the time were grimly determined to carry out the deep strike missions being planned, but concerns about the many challenges posed by the missions run deep.*

What were those challenges that shadowed the initial confidence in the mission?

Firstly, weather hindered the ability of the helicopter to operate. High-density altitude around mountainous terrain restricted the weight the AH-64 could carry. Secondly, Apache *missions were not easy to fly and to plan. Thirdly, the* Apache *was designed to support ground troops. Therefore, it was difficult to use it in the ground role when there were no ground troops to protect. Lastly, political pressures to keep casualties low or even worse, to suffer no casualties.*

According to information obtained from Army Times, 1999, the aviators of the 11th Aviation regiment, which supplied Task Force Hawk Apaches, *and the 12th Aviation Brigade, from which the Task Force's UH-60* Black Hawks *and CH-47* Chinooks *support helicopters were drawn. The base spent the week since their arrival running through MREs, meals ready to eat, in this case, anything but mission rehearsal exercises. Army Times correspondents flew on occasions such missions.*

Night Operations

During those rehearsals, Colonel Jeff Scholoesser, commander of the 12th Aviation Brigade, debriefed Army Times correspondents. Apache practice missions involved two groups of aircraft, called packs. A heavy pack (large) and a light pack (small). Such packs were taken from the same squadron, typically either 2nd or 6th squadrons of the 6th U.S. Cavalry. A Black Hawk command and control aircraft supported each pack, with a field commander controlling the combat and maintaining communications with the rear and with other aircraft. The two packs, heavy and light were flown at a distance from each other in the order of miles, thus allowing the Apache to attack targets of opportunity. Also, like in Vietnam, other helicopters are on station only minutes away to rescue any downed aircrew.

The missions were flown at night to provide cover from Serbian spotters. The Apache at night is difficult to see, even in a full moon it may appear like a black shadow easily camouflaged against the mountains, according to Apache pilots. The weather was the determining factor in making a go/no-go decision. If any action had taken place, the multiple launch rocket system of the 1st Battalion, 27th Field Artillery Regiment would have been first to draw blood, not the Apache, according to Army officials. The U.S. Army had MLRS launchers that can fire Tactical Missiles to suppress Serbian Air Defense sites that could pose a threat to the approaching Apaches.

Flying at night, just a few hundred feet above the terrain, following river valleys, in between mountains, as their only cover was a very demanding proposition for any Apache pilot. Particularly, this planned tactic to protect the Apache, created communication problems between the Packs and the command centers, in the air and on the ground. Therefore, it was an obstacle that kept Task Force Hawk from reporting mission's progress. A problem that was never solved. According to Colonel Jeff Schloesser, the mountainous terrain also challenged the skills of the pilots and capabilities of their aircraft, Colonel Schloesser said:

..."this is tough terrain, very difficult, it reminds me of Korea."

According to Task Force Hawk officials, pilots blamed "terrain" for the April 26 crash. In essence, officials said that the aircraft did not have enough power to do what the pilots wanted it to do in the thin air of the mountains. The Apache was loaded down with ammunition and fuel, including an auxiliary fuel tank. Therefore, in spite of the pilot's best efforts the Apache crashed, and was completely destroyed but miraculously the two-crew members escaped unharmed.

In examining the causes of the crash, one can see that was a warning sign for the Task Force. Any aviator operating in a war theatre is at risk flying through mountainous

terrain. But proper planning can minimize risk. Pilots of the Task Force Hawk trained for flying at sea level in Germany without full weapons, payload and/or auxiliary tanks. On this issue, Colonel Paul Wood, 11th Aviation Regiment Executive Officer said that:

..."It is easy to figure out what your power constraints are on paper, but these weights and these altitudes are not conditions under which we have habitually flown."

That shows flaws in Army training, specially pilots, who from the start in their aviation careers, should know more about density altitude and weight and balance for their own aircraft than a private pilot at the local flying club. The accident showed they were not ready, the Army lost a helicopter, according to the author, it was lack of planning, in other words, "pilot error".

The options after the accident were simple. Firstly, to reduce the weapon loads for the mission. Secondly, to reduce the amount of fuel on board, thus reducing range. Lastly, was to take off without fuel tanks and then refuel them en route to Kosovo as stated by Colonel Woods, using forward area as a refueling point. That could have created a compromising situation, since the operation would have required depending on fuel laden Chinooks, *called "fat cows" landing somewhere close to* the Apache's *route to refuel them. Having the* Apache *and the* Chinook *side by side on the ground would have been an inviting target for* Serbian *troops. The above mentioned options did not work because, according to* Colonel Wood, *smaller weapon payload could have required more helicopters for the same mission and being down o the ground for an hour or so would have depended on how far into* Kosovo *they had to go. Without knowing the terrain, weather, and time frame, these actions could have proven disastrous for the* Task Force Hawk. *Rehearsal exercises showed that each of the Apache squadrons flew simu-lated missions inside* Kosovo *from Northern Albania. The idea behind these rehearsals was to fly low, penetrate hostile territory, attack targets of opportunity and return back to base with each squadron taking turns for the mission. Apache squadrons, had the capability to destroy a* Serbian *regiment, a brigade size force in a single mission, according to a* Task Force Hawk *source familiar with deep operations.*

Many aviators in the Task Force *were concerned about using the* Apache *to conduct deep strikes into* Kosovo. *One official said, that the* Apache *was developed to be used in support of divisions on the ground. A typical Apache mission would involve friendly ground troops attacking enemy forces, forcing those enemy elements to react to the offensive. The* Apaches *would then be used to "ambush" enemy columns as they move to resist the ground attack. The problem was that in* Kosovo *there were no ground troops to support. One Aviation Officer said:*

"How do you ambush someone who is hiding? That's our dilemma."

There was a misconception in the use of the Apache *from* Task Force *commanders. Firstly, the* Apache *deep strike operation were not linked to a ground troop units, thus* Task Force *officials refuted the suggestions by say-ing that, ignoring manoeuvres in favor of fire power was not what they believed. One officer said:*

"We truly believe the Apaches are a manoeuvre force, just like a ground force."

The U.S. Army rationale was that the Apache acted primarily as an anti-tank killer, the deep operation missions could also have been used to attack command and control centers as well as anti-personnel weapons systems. However, the official said that the Apache would not loiter over, rather trolling for targets.

Why? Because they could have become the targets themselves, one expert said:

'You don't troll with Apaches, it is a bad way to use the Apache, they are ineffective and they could become vulnerable."

Nothing could be further from the truth. Low flying Apaches were extremely vulnerable to automatic air defense weapons, shoulder-fired missiles such as the SA-7 and even small arms fire. This meaning the Task Force was aware of the risk of air defense ambushes in which the Serbian troops left an inviting target in the open for the Apache to attack. Thus, surround it with hidden short-range air defense systems and automatic weapons, same way it was done in Vietnam thirty years ago.

The U.S. Army knew that air defense ambushes were a risk, the Task Force officers were keenly aware of the personal and political risks associated with the mission, one commander said:

"We can't afford to have anybody hit…we know it would be tough on our national will."

Why were they deployed? Task Force Hawk in spite of suffering from logistics and operational problems as stated before, it was simply not ready.

According to Brigadier General Dick Cody, one of the Army's most experienced and respected aviators, the aviation force was not broken, but it mustn't change the way it developed aviation officers, because many of today's platoon, company and battalion level commanders do not know what right looks like. Brigadier General Cody's comments went all the way up to Army Chief of Staff General Eric Shinseki. In his comments Brig. General Cody emphasized:

"I want to make it clear that I do not think we are broke…in fact, the aviation soldiers of Task Force Hawk performed superbly, under some of the toughest conditions I have seen in twenty seven years."

Also, Cody's message highlighted several problems seen during the Task Force deployment including inexperienced pilots and commanders, lack of state of the art night vision equipment and inadequate logistics. However, Chief of Staff General Shinseki who regarded the problem as an indication of readiness problem in the aviation branch did not take Cody's message seriously. In an Army Times interview conducted on June 24, General Shinseki told that despite the history of problems outlined in the memo, it was interpreted by some as a finger point at aviation readiness. Also, General Shinseki treated the memo the way that anybody would treat it coming out of an after-action review. But Brigadier General Cody is an experienced and well-known Army Aviator. He has 5,000 flying hours under his belt and combat duty during the 1991 Persian Gulf War, in which he led the deep attack that knock out Iraqi air defense sites on the opening night of the war. Cody's review of Task Force Hawk *was not supposed to be taken lightly as Chief of Staff General Shinseki put it. Army Times records show that when* Task Force*

Hawk was formed in early April, 1999, the Army, seeking to capitalize on Cody's experience, pulled him from his job as Assistant Division Commander of the 4th Infantry Division (mechanized) at Fort Hood, Texas and made him the Task Force Deputy Commander General. Cody's primary responsibility was to supervise* Task Force Hawk's *deep strike* Apache *raids. According to Cody's report, Apache units were so short of warrant officers, who made up the bulk of the pilot community, that 11 crews had to be sent over from Fort Bragg, NC. Also, sources from the 11th Aviation regiment, Illesheim, Germany, to which the squadron belong, told Army Times that each squadron could only man 16 or 17 of its 24 helicopters. The regiment left 24 of its 48 Apaches behind in Germany when it deployed to Albania. That is 50 percent deployment and 60 percent readiness. Talking about pilots, 65 percent of the pilots had less than 500 hours* *in the cockpit and none were qualified to use night vision goggles in the Apache's co-pilot gunner position, according to Cody's report.*

By motives probably beyond his military career, General Shinseki did not want to see Cody's concerns about the experience level of the commissioned officers that commanded Apache units. Also, Brigadier General Cody expressed concerns that none of the lieutenants who had just left platoon command had achieved pilot-in-command status and neither had any of the current troop commanders. Cody said that:

"The bottom line, from my perspective is that we are not growing our young aviation leaders well enough in the first 3 years after flight school…the results are young captains emerging from the advanced course with little flight experience and little aviation savvy on what right looks like going into command."

Cody also warned in his report that:

"This approach carries serious risks, most importantly, we are placing them and their units at risk when we have to ramp up for a real world crisis."

On a final note, Cody supported Task Force Hawk *in saying that after 16 missions rehearsals exercises in Albania, saying that he would put the* Task Force Hawk *pilots and commanders up against anyone, but it was painful and high risk during the first three weeks. Cody also recommended not allowing commanders to pull lieutenants out of platoon command and assign them to staff jobs before lieutenants had achieved pilot-in-command status and have flown more than 500 hours. His final note like this:*

"This is clearly a leadership and command issue…right now we are at a crucial time in our branch history, because we know have several young lieutenant colonels coming up into command who were never pilot-in-command, have less than 1,000 hours of flight time and they are the ones developing the next group…and they do not know what right looks like either."

General Shinseki's comments wrongfully implied that Cody's concerns were routine after action reports, General Shinseki said:

"It is a self-critique to make us better at it the next time."

In the author's point of view, it is more than a concern, it is likely fact! Brigadier General Cody also stated that:

"We would always like to have pilots with far more hours in the cockpit as you cross the line of departure."

On the night equipment, the Apache is equipped with a forward-looking infrared (FLIR) night-vision system in which objects are distinguished from each other depending on how much heat they emit. But this system does not function properly in all weather conditions, and many pilots prefer their co-pilot gunners to wear night-vision goggles that use available light, rather than heat. Brigadier General Cody wrote that:

"Recent history has shown us that every time we have a real world, high-risk mission we have nits scrambling to get their co-pilot gunners qualified on night-vision goggles for mission success and for safety enhancement…in Albania, with its rugged terrain, poorly marked power lines and unpredictable weather patterns, relying solely on FLIR was not a good option."

However, according to reports from Army Times, the 11th regiment pilots had not trained on goggles for the better part of two years, and had none in their inventory. Army Times reported that, Cody ordered goggles for the crews, who then had to fit in a training program for their co-pilot gunners at the same time as they were conducting mission rehearsal exercises. But according to Cody, the effort was worth it.

"I reviewed several hours of cockpit video of the mission rehearsal exercises and I am convinced that if it were not for night-vision goggles in the co-pilot gunner position, we would have sustained several wire strikes and possible one or two mid-air collisions."

Brig. General Cody was also critical of the Aviation Restructure Initiative that reorganized the Army's aviation units beginning in 1993 in this way:

"Early on Task Force Hawk determined that neither the 11th Aviation Regiment, the two squadrons and the corps deep operations control cell had enough aviation staff officers to simultaneously plan, rehearse and execute the current mission and the upcoming missions…Task Force Hawk is not an anomaly, we have been robbing Peter to pay Paul for quite some time since we implemented the Aviation Restructure Initiative."

The responsibility of the outcome of the Apache mission does not rest with the aircrews, whose motivation and courage were beyond doubt, according to the author. It rests higher on the command chain. The failure of the mission lies on the AH-64 misuse. It can be attributed to mismanagement from higher rank officers who failed to provide our policy decision makers with the true facts, capabilities and options to use and deploy available technology from the U.S. arsenal in this case the AH-64 Apache. Also, it failed in listening to experienced aviators like Brigadier General Cody who knew the job best.

The overall evaluation of the Apache's mission over Kosovo can be considered, with the loss of 2 ships, 2 crewmembers, millions of dollars in supporting logistics and no-results, hardly a success. Why then was the Apache deployed? It can be said that the small deployment of helicopters was done to create a psychological deterrent to Serbian troops on the ground. As a military option, it clearly made no-sense, not by itself. Twenty-four helicopters did not provide a sufficient force to increase NATO's striking potential and as a deterrence force, the frightful though of B-52s flying over Belgrade, would have been much more powerful deterrent.

Knowing the internal problems in logistics, training and operational management, deploying the Apache under those conditions was one of the worst decisions made by top Army officers since the Vietnam War. Army's pride at the highest levels prevented them from admitting lack of readiness and inadequacy of the helicopter for that kind of operation, so ready or not the Army deployed the Apache to Kosovo.

According to Army Times report published on 08-16-99, on April 7 four days after the Task Force was ordered to Albania, U.S. Defense Secretary William Cohen met with NATO General Wesley Clark in Belgium. There,

Cohen told reporters that General Clark would receive what he needs in order to carry out this campaign successfully. But according to Pentagon and NATO sources the permission to send the Apache into combat never came. In other words, the Defense Department backed by the Army failed to live up to that promise.

In an interview with Army Times *on July 5, 1999 General Clark said that he ask for permission to deploy an* Apache Task Force *on March 24, thinking that the helicopters would be very useful in going after the Serbian ground forces in Kosovo. General Clark had no uninformed military officers above him in his U.S. chain of command, which run straight from him to Defense Secretary William Cohen to President Clinton. The White House delegated authority for approving Clark's request to Cohen, according to sources with the Joint Chiefs of Staff and NATO. According to* Army Times, *Cohen, was reluctant to make any decision on the Task Force without getting the nod from Joint Chiefs of Staff Chairman General Henry Shelton. After a rather heated debate, the Joint Chiefs of Staff acquiesced to the deployment of* Task Force Hawk, *but withheld the authority to commit the* Apaches *to battle.*

The Pentagon's reservations centered on three issues. Firstly, a perception that missions weren't worth the risk to the aircrews. Secondly, that a fear of Tactical Missile System strikes would precede the Apache *missions would hit civilians. Lastly, a concern that using the* Apache *and ATACMS would fundamentally alter the character of a war that until then NATO had chosen to wage from 15,000 ft.*

When Clark's request for the Apaches *came, it took the Joint Chiefs of Staff by surprise,* Army Times *reported. A suspicion quickly developed that General Clark and his staff had not thought through their plans. In fact General Clark never provided the detailed briefing on the proposed* Apache *missions requested by the Joint Chiefs of Staff.* (www.mco.com/mem/archives/army/1999)

After the war the controversy of using the Apache *in Kosovo continued. General Clark still asserted that the* Apaches *could have done the job.*

General Clark told Army Times that the helicopters were extremely capable, and could have done the job effectively. However, General Clark declined to comment on his discussions with the Pentagon over Task Force Hawk, but others familiar with the debate said he was troubled by the constraints placed on him, and by the Army leadership's role in denying him the use of the Apaches. General Clark was deeply disappointed by the whole affair, the NATO officer said. On July 27, General Clark paid for his tenacity. Joint Chiefs Chairman General Henry Shelton informed General Clark that he was, in essence, being forced to retire early. General Clark was a 33-year veteran, was asked to leave his post in April, 1999, two months ahead of schedule. General Joseph Ralston, an Air Force Officer, replaced General Clark as Supreme Commander of NATO and chief of the U.S. European Command.

Chapter V
Assessment

Since the beginning of April 1999, NATO has conducted an intensive air campaign against the *Serbs*. Many people asserted that the air campaign in *Yugoslavia* has not been effective. That was a premature and incorrect statement.

According to General Michael E. Ryan, Air Force Chief of Staff, the campaign did not begin the way that America normally would apply air power, massively, striking at strategic centers of gravity that support *Milosevic* and his oppressive regime. General Clark initially believed that tactically constrained air attacks on dispersed infantry force, brutishly looting and burning villages, could alone halt the atrocities or reverse the refugee flow, as stated by General Ryan. But military officials were convinced that such actions could and will destroy the army that has perpetrated those acts.

NATO conducted a summit in Washington, almost a month into the air campaign, by then it became clear to NATO that General Clark's constraints and initial approach were not effective. At the insistence of U.S. leaders, General Short among then, NATO widened the air campaign to produce the right strategic effects on *Yugoslavia*. The result started to become more obvious. According to General Ryan, *Serbia's* air force was essentially useless and its air defenses were dangerous but ineffective. Military armament production was destroyed, military supply areas were under siege, Oil refinement has ceased and petroleum storage was systematically being destroyed. Electricity was sporadic, at best. Major transportation routes were out. Local media showed that NATO aircraft were attacking with impunity throughout the country. With the continued build-up of NATO aircraft and better weather, the attacks were intensifying and the effects were mounting. Also, it was evident that, weakening in the *Yugoslavian* military and police forces were widening. Draftees were failing to report for duty; unit desertions were on the rise. Protests against the regime were increasing and *Serbian* civilian leaders were calling for a settlement.

On a media interview, President Clinton said that:

"He can cut his losses now and accept the basic requirements of a just peace, or he can continue to force military failure and economic ruin on his people. In the end, the outcome will be the same."

General Ryan stated that, this air campaign was executed with great precision and with great valor by NATO forces. Admittedly, we have had instances of collateral damage and unintended loss of life, but they were few and inadvertent. General Ryan also expressed that NATO forces went to great lengths to avoid harming innocent people, in fact, NATO aircrews often put themselves at greater risk just to minimize it. General Ryan said that:

> *"Our forces have seen firsthand the destruction Milosevic has perpetrated against his own people in Kosovo solely because of their ethnicity and religion. We must stay the course, We know NATO's mission is just and NATO's actions justifiable, and we know NATO's forces will prevail.(Washington Post, June 4, 1999)*

There were other officials who also shared General Ryan's optimism. Like Jim Garamone, *American Forces Press Service* who reported that allied air operations in *Yugoslavia* pounded fuel depots, *Serbian* command and control facilities, air defenses sites and *Yugoslavian* army and special police units. Also, that NATO airstrikes destroyed the headquarters of the 3rd Army, the unit conducting ethnic cleansing in *Kosovo*.

Including in these airstrikes were the brigade headquarters of both the Pristina Corps and the Nis Corps of the 3rd Yugoslavian Army.

In essence, NATO attacks degraded President Slobodan Milosevic's ability to make war. Rear Admiral Tom Wilson, the Joint Staff Director of Intelligence, said that NATO forces targeted fuel depots hitting approximately 30 out of 100 of them. Rear Admiral *Wilson* also said that NATO planners targeted bridges and roads along *Yugoslavian* lines of communication from *Serbia* to *Kosovo*. The rationale behind these attacks was to choke off supplies to the *Serbs* forces conducting the ethnic cleansing campaign.

During the beginning of the air campaign, NATO aircraft, mainly B-2 *Stealth Bombers*, were attacking primarily high-value targets that were mostly easy to find, including command and communication centers, integrated air defense systems, weapons factories and military storage sites. According to reports from Paul Richter, Times Staff Writer, NATO went after those targets with intense firepower during the first sorties hopping to swiftly destroying some of *Yugoslavian* President Slobosdan Molosevic's most important military targets. But, airstrikes triggered a secondary effect, that of new massacres in *Kosovo*. Tom Watson, Times Staff Writer, stated that instead of bombing *Yugoslavia* back to the bargaining table, *NATO's* airstrikes provoked new massacres and terrorist attacks in *Kosovo*, according to ethnic *Albanians* sources. *Serbian* atrocities raised more doubt on weather NATO airpower was enough to stop a civil war that inflicted point-blank executions as well as long range artillery on a largely un-armed people. And at the same time, on the other hand, NATO aircraft were hitting the wrong targets. Paul Watson reported this in the Los Angeles Times that cluster bombs may be what killed refugees in a *Kosovo* road. Evidence of craters and mysterious fin-shaped pieces of metal found next to civilian vehicles attacked in *Kosovo* suggested that they were hit by U.S. cluster bombs designed to destroy tanks. This kind of evidence was also found at different sites over a number of days. Evidence showed that the intact bomb remnants, shaped like single fins about two feet long with one-inch hole at one end, were stamped in two places with the name *ALCOA*, suggesting that the U.S. Aluminum Company made them. The Pentagon made a statement that one type of cluster bomb used in *Kosovo*, was a high-tech, heat seeking bomb that hasn't been used before.

In spite of NATO's initial successes, as stated by General Wesley Clark, NATO supreme commander, and according to Times reports, NATO bombers scored several direct hits in Pristina, *Kosovo's* capital including a graveyard, a bus station and a children's basketball court. General Clark stressed that almost all his pilots' weapons were precision guided, so-called smart bombs and that almost without exception, the targets were very precisely struck. General Clark repeatedly reassured that the North Atlantic Treaty Organization was not at war with the people of *Yugoslavia* in spite of current results. But on May 9, 1999 one or a series of bombs stuck the *Chinese* embassy in *Belgrade* sending the *Chinese* people into furies.

China's foremost newspaper, the *People's Party*, stressed any attempt to intimidate the *Chinese* with force would prove futile and warned that the U.S. led-*NATO* will commit a historical mistake if it ignores the *Chinese* people's indignation at its barbaric attacks against the *Chinese* embassy in *Yugoslavia*. The commentary, entitled *"The Chinese People Are Not to be Humiliated"*, said the *Chinese* government. They issued a stern statement on the same day stating that as the savage act occurred, most strongly protesting NATO's crime of barbarically infringing the *Chinese* sovereignty and brutally ravaging *China's* dignity. The *Chinese* also urged NATO to bear all responsibilities arising therefrom and stressing the reservation of its right to take further action on the matter, according to *China News*. The commentary believed powerful and prosperous *China* with its entire people and nationalities united in one heart, was the guarantee for the *Chinese* nation's existence and prosperity. Also, the commentary adamantly stated that *China's* sovereignty and national dignity allow no aggression and the *Chinese* people, who are not afraid of hegemony, will tolerate no bullying from others. The more than a century's arduous struggle of the *Chinese* nation has, and will continue to prove that the great *Chinese* nation is invincible. They stated that if the U.S. led-NATO turns a blind eye to *Chinese* people's indignation, it is doomed to make a huge mistake and will never go away unpunished. But was it really a mistake?

London's Sunday Times, reported on May 9, 1999 that the *Chinese* Embassy was on the target list. *British* analysts noticed that there was confusion around the explanation how the *Chinese* Embassy in *Belgrade* happened to be bombarded raised serious doubts in motives and background of this tragic event. *British* analysts were totally unconvinced about the explanation offered by *Brussels* raised doubts that bombarding of the *Chinese* Embassy has no direct connection with NATO as a whole, but with *American* administration which attempted to utilize growing tension with *China* for its local political purpose. Also the analysts doubted that three missiles fired at the embassy were not a "catastrophic mistake" as first officially stated, but pure intention. According to their best estimates the embassy was purposely targeted. The analysts view is shared by the author in the sense that the *Chinese* Embassy bombing was not actually a mistake by the aircrew but rather by U.S. war planners, who apparently mistakenly though they were striking a military supply center several hundred yards away. A mistake? Possibly, however, the bombing coincides, right after the time in which the *Chinese* were discovered stealing U.S. top-secret nuclear data.

London Sunday Times is the only source that pointed out that lethal missiles, it looked like, were launched by American bombers like the B-2. In the First NATO statement, according to the *Times*, it was told that the embassy had been hit by mistake and that the actual target had been the other building in its vicinity. In a special statement later on it was told that it was not the pilot's mistake but the embassy was, allegedly by mistake, put in the target list.

Some specialists for these issues, however, believe that the attack on the embassy has practically discovered the existence of a special plan in the aggression on *Yugoslavia,* carried only by the U.S.A. with aims different than those proclaimed by *NATO* command. The fact was that special units of the *American Strategic Aviation,* which was not subordinated, committed the bombarding, to NATO and which landed off from the American territory could only support these assumptions. The *Sunday Times* launched a story later the same week that the real aim was *"Yugoslavia"* hotel, hit the same night. In NATO headquarters at the same time it was told that the target had been the "command of military forces", but it was not precisely told which command was in question.

Another explanation from the Pentagon and NATO was that the bombarding of the *Chinese* Embassy was the consequence of "wrong information of spies from *Belgrade"*, according to which the embassy building was storage of weapons and ammunition. Obviously the Pentagon tried to cast their guilt to spy network and thus they say that the information was maybe received from a double spy. However, *London* and *Washington* know exactly where the *Chinese* Embassy is located at, and any possible mistake in locating it is not a very supportive explanation.

The *London Sunday Times*, the military analyst and the Ministry of Information in *London* suspect the American CIA was behind the bombing. Many *British* analysts were convinced in as they did not believe that the embassy was bombarded due to wrong information from a double spy, but due to special plans of the *CIA* which practically misused NATO. The *London's Sunday Times* recalls that General Wesley Clark was the only one who knew the whole story, the real truth. Being the Allied Supreme Commander carries a direct responsibility in focusing a further investigation on.

On a Department of Defense Briefing held on Saturday, May 8, 1999 at 11:05 a.m., Assistant Secretary Mr. Kenneth H. Bacon, stated that there is no such thing as clean combat and that NATO had the best pilots, the best weapons in the world, the best planned missions and the best trained forces. Also, the secretary commented that there was no way to avoid collateral damage or unintended consequences when weapons were employed to solve what might have been solved diplomatically. Secretary Bacon put it succinctly as:

…"we deeply regret the loss of life at the Chinese embassy last night in Belgrade. We did not target that building. The bombing was in error. It is currently under review by NATO, and when that review is complete, NATO will have more to say about what happened. I can't go beyond what NATO said except to re-stress that this was a mistake. We deeply regret it, and we express our condolences to the Chinese for the diplomats who died and were injured in the attack."

However, Assistant Secretary Bacon, there is no evidence in his speech that he apologized to the *Chinese* Government in any way. In fact Mr. Bacon did not apologize.

The Air Force Viewpoint

The Air Force personnel were far from the political arena that surrounded the bombing of the *Chinese* Embassy in *Belgrade.* Linda D. Kozaryn, from the American Forces Press Service, interviewed maintenance crews, support crews, pilots from their station in *Aviano Air Base* in *Italy.* Some of the comments that Kozaryn obtained from Aviano's were:

"We are supporting sorties morning, noon and night."
Said 1st Lt. Jeff Styers, U.S. Air Force 23rd Fighter Squadron
"We catch them, we fix them, then we load them and we launch them."
Said the maintenance officer from Clarksville, Va.

The enthusiasm and dedication was evident, the Air Force had a lot of well trained specialists and crew chiefs working on their aircraft, weapons load crews backing them up showing what training, during the previous 12 months, can do. The overall feeling from the pilots coming back from missions was that they were there with the sole motivation to stop the massacres and the inhumanity that went on. That kept the pilots motivated. They worked long hours, the morale was high and when they watched television and saw the refugees and that reinforced what they were there to do.

Senior Master Sgt. Jeanie Thompson. From Danville, Ill., was among 23 reservists from the 184th Services Flight, Kansas Air National Guard deployed to Aviano for two weeks. The unit provided food, lodging, recreation, field laundry management, mortuary and other support services, she said:

We feel lucky to be at the base during allied forces contingency…this is what we trained to do. We are actually happy to be able to do our job even if it is only for a short period of time."

Overall, about 7,300 *American* and 6,000 NATO service members along with 230 U.S. and 220 NATO planes support NATO air operations. The number of personnel and aircraft involved kept going up as U.S. Army General Wesley Clark, operation commander called for more air power and other assets.

The NATO mission "clearly had an impact" on U.S. pilots and crews who were already supporting *Operation Northern* and *Southern Watch* over *Iraq, Operation Deny Flight* over *Bosnia* and other real world missions, according to U.S. Air Force General Joseph Ralston. The Vice-Chairman of the Joint Chiefs of Staff said that *AWACs*, EA-6B *Prowlers* and other high demand, low-density weapons systems were actually, indispensable. General Ralston added after visiting an air base in April:

"We have looked to see if there are other commitments that they can be reduced…we are canceling exercises, for example, that they would do right now that they can get on without the mission."

NATO aimed to accomplish its *Allied Force* mission, effectively and efficiently, with as little risk as possible to pilots, crews and aircraft, according to U.S. Air Force Lt. Colonel William T. Eliason, 603rd Air Control Squadron commander. Working with Aviano's *Italian* air controllers and others, the squadron helped give pilots the information they needed to make that happen. An air battle manager from Allentown, Pa., said:

"Our job is to help get to the tankers, get into the target area, return to the tankers and get back to base safely, regardless of weather…it is a difficult process to put this many airplanes in the air and bring them home safely."

Also, General Eliason said that today's computers provide an unprecedented degree of control and accuracy:

"Consider what we had in World war Two, manual telephones, very primitive radar and bombing systems. We would have to send hundreds of B-17s and thousands of bombs to get to one target. We're now down to almost one target, one bomb, with very limited collateral damage. Without computers it would be impossible."

NATO pilots were achieving their objectives each time they went out. So far, only one aircraft has been lost, a U.S. F-117 *Nighthawk Stealth Fighter*. Safety was the top priority according to General Eliason, he also said:

"Because we need each and every one of those airplanes back, in the same condition, hopefully, as we sent them out in, so we can send them back up."

As far as the weather was concerned, General Eliason, said that it was not as frustrating as the press originally stated it. The General's opinion reflected the view that it was possible to attack targets in a variety of weather conditions, but he added:

"Adverse weather has had an impact, because pilots were operating at high altitudes to avoid Serbian threats, they have been unable to see targets due to low visibility."

General Eliason further explained in his interview with Linda Kozaryn that:

"It is still pretty much visual game where the pilot has to see what he is going to shoot at. If you are asking him to drop his weapon on a

military target and not miss,…then he needs to be able to visually verify the target before he releases the weapon. It's upwards of 2,000 pounds of explosives that you want to place right on that target and not on somebody's back yard."

In this area, General Eliason also said that *Yugoslavia* is much different *from Dessert Storm* in which *Iraq's* desert is a not *Yugoslavia's* mountain:

"The enemy is not easily distinguishable as it was in desert Storm. So we have to be very careful when we roll in on those targets to make sure we see what we were shooting at is what we were told by intelligence to go after."

General Eliason's statements could provide an insight on how target were selected the night the *Chinese* Embassy was bombed.

General Eliason also noted that *Yugoslavia* is smaller than *Red Flag* training ranges at Nellis Air Force Base, Nevada, where U.S. and NATO pilots practice air war fighting skills:

"Kosovo is about the size of Rhode Island and Connecticut put together. You know what it is like to fly into Providence, well imagine trying to throw 80 airplanes at one time into that one space."

Red Flag exercises kept allied pilots well tuned for this kind of environment, said one F-15E weapons systems officer, identified only as *"Jim"* due to security concerns. According to information from Linda Kozaryn, *Jim* flew combat air patrols and air-ground missions equipped with laser-guided bombs. *Red Flag* was more even difficult than the real thing, he noted, because the opponents at Nellis "knew where you were at, *Jim* said:

"Everyone in the air force trains to a high standard of self-defense."

On another pilot's view, *John* and F-16CJ pilot said:

"Everyone on their toes, you put in 12 hours a day, if you are not flying, you are doing mission planning, scheduling and other support around the squad room, Serb air defense forces were intelligent, it was not a cake walk."

Based on the above comments, it can be said that the U.S. Air Force operated over *Kosovo* in a safe and accurate manner.

Chapter VI
Views of the Air Campaign

In a *Los Angeles Times* article published on July 8, 1999 by Rolin Wright Times Staff writer commented on the air power ability to win wars and the failure to purge *"Rogue Leaders"*. In his opinion, *Wright* said that after 78 days of air strikes and 34,300 sorties, the U.S. and its allies appeared to have curbed the flagrant aggression of *Yugoslavian* President Slobodan Milosevic. But, they have not managed to exit him from power. Something the Air Campaign did not intend to do *(emphasis added)*.

Wright's view is accurate in bearing an uncomfortable resemblance to the former *Gulf War* against *Iraq*. According to Wright, the U.S. and its allies were able in 1991 to reverse *Iraqi* President Saddam Hussein's invasion of *Kuwait*. But eight years and 250,000 sorties later, Hussein's stubborn standoff with the West shows no sign of ending soon. Wright's political view supports the bitter afterstate of the *Persian Gulf War* in which appears to be one reason why the NATO's victory in *Yugoslavia* does not seem quite as sweet as it might be otherwise.

Wright's military assessment was right only in the sense that in both theatres, *Iraq* and *Yugoslavia,* a fundamental lesson is clear. Allied air power can deter or defeat military aggression, making a ground offensive comparatively easy or even unnecessary.

Wright also questioned that the thunderous might of aerial bombardment was not effective in removing an authoritarian leader from power, at least not with any speed. In this case, Wright's assessment was incorrect in the following sense. Firstly, Milosevic's government palace was, for some reason, not bombed. Secondly, air power over *Yugoslavia* was politically driven hindering its effective use. Wright also stated that airstrikes have not proved to be a useful political tool. Of course not, strategic bombing is a pure military action, not political *(emphasis added)*.

Some senior *U.S.* officials acknowledged that bombing could only put on additional pressure on governments. But Michael Einsenstadt, an expert at the Washington Institute for Near East Policy, said that:

"The right people aren't being hit, so is not going to result in a decisive strategic outcome."

However, Washington hoped that the ongoing allied bombardments could tighten the squeeze and eventually prod the military or civilians to act against Milosevic. General Charles Horner, retired *Gulf War* Commander on *Waging Air Strikes*, said on March 24 in an interview with *ABC News* that:

"I think the emphasis will shift to attack on air defenses to hitting military targets, primarily Serbian army and special police forces in Kosovo."

Horner, in a way, supported General Clark's view on the bombing campaign. However, chasing troops on the ground was not part of efficient strategic bombing as previously proved in former wars. During the same interview, General Horner was asked if he believed that air power alone was going to remedy the situation, the general replied:

"Often the air power is conducted in conjunction with other factors, certainly in this case, a heavy dose of diplomatic negotiation. So, of course, air power alone will not remedy the situation. It may be the only military force we have available for use, given the nebulous national security objectives and our people unwilling to incur large casualties…in view of those limited objectives."

In Horner's view on the capabilities of Mig's and other jets vs. NATO aircraft, General Horner said that:

"Serbian Air Force aircraft could be a serious threat. They had capable performance and reasonable air to air weapons. But, they were no match

for advanced radars and air-to-air missiles of aircraft such as NATO's F-16s. In addition, NATO pilots were backed up by airborne warning and control aircraft (AWACS), which tracked Serbian fighters the minute they took off. Given the situational awareness, and tools NATO pilots had, the outcome…is a pretty uneven fight."

Also, General Horner stated the use of the B-2 in the war by saying that:

"The B-2 represented the most advanced capability in our inventory. I was surprised that only 2 sorties were flown, because this system has the capability to destroy 16 Hardened targets on one pass with complete immunity from the Serbian defenses. If you think, it's a powerful argument for Milosevic to make a peace agreement."

One of the questions passed to General Horner was, if he thought this campaign (meaning *Allied Force*) could turn into another *Vietnam*, Horner replied:

"Well, I don't think this situation will be anything like Vietnam, in terms of large numbers of friendly casualties. The disturbing part of this crisis is that it is going to require many, many years of involvement to preclude the ethnic strife from breaking out again. Well, given the goal to disarm the Serbians, the bombings will work to some extent." *"Whether or not they can force the Serbs to agree to some sort of peace keeping force is another question. But one way they may work is, they buy time, or the KLA be able of defending ethnic Albanians from the Serbs. That would mean the fighting will continue but the aspects of genocide would be reduced."*

General Horner shied away from answering the question, "was progressive involvement and deployment, including politically selected targets in fact the making of *Vietnam* all over?

Despite the dedication, effort, valor and enthusiasm demonstrated by NATO armed forces, operation *Allied Force* was shadowed by criticism, and political opinions from individuals that, as it seems, were against military intervention. Richard N. Haas, Director of Foreign Policy Studies said to The Washington Post on April 19, 1999 that:

"NATO-Clinton Administration policy toward Kosovo can be captured in just four words, ambitious objectives, modest means."

The Washignton Post staff, officers or members of the Brooking Institution did, not share the views expressed by Richard Haas. However, besides Haas's political view of the campaign, there are a few interested points that could be considered starting points for future discussion. On a first count, according to Haas, the military force being used was simply inadequate to the task and weeks or even months of more bombing was unlikely to resolve the problem. On a second count, strategic bombing tended to lose impact over time, as misery becomes a fact of life, tactical bombing of units and equipment advanced slowly. The results of the air campaign clearly contradict Haas's two counts, (www.brook.edu/views/op-ed/haas/19990419.htm).

Another objective view of the air campaign was done by Rear Admiral Eugene J. Carroll Jr., USN (Ret), Deputy Director for The Center for Defense Information. Carroll's article appeared in Newsday, on March 26, 1999, in it Carroll sated that"

"military action cannot resolve the issues that underlie the violence in Kosovo. There is simply no military solution to the complex historic, ethnic and religious issues motivating the conflict there. And, even if there were one, it could not be accomplished from the air alone."(www.cdi.org/weekly/1999/issue13.html)

The admiral went on to say in is article that missiles, and bombs, no matters how smart they may be, are blunt, brutal instruments of destruction that intensify and deepen wounds-rather than healing them. Also, he added that bombing would not change the political reality of *Serbian* control in *Kosovo*. Admiral Carroll added to his comments that NATO bombing could tighten Milosevic authoritarian grip in *Serbia*, that historically aerial bombardment consistently does not create political opposition to remove governments from power and that the cost in financing the war was not worth it. Real Admiral Carroll forgets in his comments the lessons from history.

Lessons from Billy Mitchell, who showed the Navy that an airplane could actually sink a ship, or the creation of the aircraft carrier versus the battleship. Or LeMay's bombing of *Japan* that made its homeland invasion unnecessary, or even the results, still surrounded by secrecy, of *Operation Linebacker II* over *Hanoi*. The invasion of the *European* continent, *Normandy*, June 6, 1944, *Dessert Storm*, and then *Operation Allied Force* were military operations to defeat aggression. Just think where we would be today if those campaigns would have failed or even worse, not even attempted.

Air Strike Assessment from General Wesley K. Clark

The purpose of General Clark's assessment of the air campaign was to present actual results to the public and to present conclusions to help the public understand precisely what was done over *Kosovo*.

From the outset of the campaign, according to General Clark, two lines of operation emerged. The first was to attack the strategic line against Serbian air defenses, command and control, *VJ* and *MUP* forces, *Serbian* infrastructure, supply routes and resources. The second, was to attack *Serbian* forces deployed in *Kosovo* and in southern *Serbia*. Initially, General Clark put the priority on the attacks against the *Serbian* forces. In his own words,

"This was imperative…we had to go on both lines of operations to be successful…and we were determined to do this even though we knew this mission was going to be extremely difficult."

Another extremely controversial part of the air campaign was the assessment of the battle damage as a way of measuring the effectiveness of air power. According to General Clark, there was some accusation toward NATO of flying too high, of not wanting to risk pilots while others chose to believe that NATO would strike only decoys or perhaps would hit nothing at all. So, how much did NATO strike? How much did NATO destroy? General Clark put it like this:

"We destroyed and struck enough. The conflict ended on NATO's terms. Serb forces are out. NATO forces are in; the refugees are home; a cease-fire is in place. So in that sense we succeeded in this conflict."

One obvious result of the campaign was that the air strikes forced the *Serb* military into hiding, thus making the attacks more difficult to do. On this issue, General Pavkovic gave NATO his own assessment of the air campaign by saying that it was insignificant. However, Pavkovic is the same General that claimed to have shot down 47 *NATO* airplanes and 4 helicopters. And as a matter of fact, that was not true (emphasis added). Unfortunately, Clark said, the media believed Pavkovic, and chose to look at evidence on the ground, and apparently listened to Pavkovic, because it turned out there were a lot of people who basically supported the Serbian claim. The following newspapers took an early conclusion by saying:

Die Welt: "*The high-flying NATO jets hardly disturbed the Serbian militias.*"

La Repubblica: "*As we drew closer to Pec, we found increasing confirmation that NATO air strikes had in fact done very little damage to Milosevic's war machine.*"

The *Sunday Telegraph:* "*The 11-week NATO bombing campaign did almost no damage to Serbian field forces in Kosovo.*"

Le Point: "*Serbian losses are not as apocalyptic as NATO is claiming.*"

The New York Times: "*Most of the tanks destroyed by NATO were already up on blocks and gathered for repairs or junking.*"

Brigadier General John Corley, Chief, Kosovo Mission Effectiveness Assessment Team mentioned, in support of General Clark, that a strike assessment of any military conflict, requires a damage assessment on the effectiveness of the munitions that were employed during the conflict. The assessment of the air campaign focused on two areas, ground mobile targets and fixed targets. At the same time there were four additional categories of mobile targets; self-propelled artillery and tanks;

armored personnel carriers or APCs; mortars and artillery and finally military vehicles.

According to Brigadier General Corley, NATO evaluated nearly 2,000 pilot reports of mobile targets in *Kosovo* alone, more than half of the targets were actually validated. In order to come to an evaluation of the strike, NATO officials looked at mission reports, on site-findings, inter-views with air controllers, cockpit videotape and pre-post strike images that included national sources as well as the U-2 including unmanned aerial vehicles like the *Predator*. Also, according to Corley's report, NATO used tactical reconnaissance after the strikes including human intelligence from *KFOR* units deployed on the ground earlier in the conflict. During the evaluation, NATO teams found decoys left by *Serbian* troops at various sites. These included artillery pieces and or vehicles. That in fact did not surprised the aircrews who, according to their own accounts, had consistently reported the decoys during their strike missions. In some instances, the pilots flew both in the morning and afternoon of the same day, and the battlefield had changed between the first and the second mission.

During the conflict, according to General Clark, NATO made exten-sive use of intelligence, surveillance and reconnaissance capabilities deployed in support of the operations. This was probably the most robust capability seen in any conflict to date.

In addition, NATO fighters had an extremely modern cockpit recording system. During this assessment both of those capabilities were analyzed extensively by the assessment team to provide the public corroborating evidence of successful strikes.

The initial figures validated by NATO as target category is concerned:

Tank category: 93 successful strikes, 19 multiple hits, and 9 decoys.

APCs: 153 successful strikes, 26 multiple hits and 5 decoys.

Military vehicles: 339 successful strikes, 37 multiple hits and 5 decoys.

Artillery pieces: 389 successful strikes, 46 multiple hits, and 6 decoys.

The final numbers then correlate to the 181 mission reports in the tank category, 317 in the APC category, 600 in the military vehicle, and 857 in the artillery and mortars.

General Clark summarized the assessment of the air campaign by saying that NATO air campaign not only destroyed fielded forces but also disabled the electrical power grid, sent its transportation infrastructure into disarray, and crippled its capability to produce and to store POL, in his words:

"The bottom line is that today in Kosovo it's beginning to return to normal. The short answer to how much did we kill, how much did we strike successfully, it was enough. The conflict ended on NATO's terms."

General *Clark* also stated that:

"This was a successful campaign. It worked."

On a press conference held on September 16, 1999 Hartwig Nathe, Focus, told General Clark that NATO Council interfered almost on a daily bases in the military operation, then asked: Do you feel this is a successful procedure? In reply, General Clark shied away from the answer by saying he had full and wholehearted support from all the elements of NATO, whatever they are, as they went against *Serbian* forces on the ground.

Doug Hamilton, Reuters said to General Clark that toward the end of the bombing campaign there was a rather dramatic incident in the Mount Pastrik region when a *B-52* reportedly caught large formations in the open on the slopes and attack them.

"Does your study tell what the results of that bombing were?"

General *Clark* replied:

"We are not going to have from a B-52 the kind of cockpit video that you'd get from dropping-precision guided weapons."

But, according to a pilot who was on the ground in *Kosovo* after the conflict to assess it, said that:

"It was truly awesome to see that level of damage in that particular very confined, very narrow area. So yes, it was pretty significant."

For the ones that know what a B-52 can do, it can be said that many *Serbian* soldiers did not return north that day (emphasis added). It is believed that B-52s surprised some 700-1,000 exposed *Serbian* troops near *Mount Pastrik* on June 7th, killing hundreds of them.

Lt. General Michael C. Short's View of the Air Campaign

John A. Tirpak, Senior Editor of Air Force Magazine interviewed Lt. General Short in September 1999, in it one can see NATO's victory in *Operation Allied Force,* according to the man who ran the air campaign. Unlike General Clark's view of the air campaign, General Short believed that what counted for most *NATO's* success in the *Balkans* was the reduction of strategic targets, not the "tank plinking " in *Kosovo.*

This strategic approach, led by Lt. General Short, paved the way for NATO's victory in the *Balkans* and may be; it was what saved NATO's defeat. According to General Short statements in his interview with John Tirpak, the massive and laborious tank pickling effort in *Kosovo* was in many ways a waste of air power since, in his opinion, it did little to achieve *NATO's* stated goals. After the initial aerial operations with little and no results, then, *NATO* shifted its tactics to attacking strategic targets in and around *Belgrade,* the capital of *Yugoslavia.* Thus, it forced *Serbian* President Slobodan Milosevic to accept NATO's terms. In his interview with John Tirpak General Short said:

"I never felt that the Serb 3rd Army in Kosovo was a center of gravity."

By center of gravity General Short meant, a force that could have played a decisive role should a NATO invasion of *Kosovo* could occur. In other words, according to Air Force doctrine, is basically an strategic asset of utmost importance, that by losing it could affect the outcome of the war in terms of capability or ability to fight.

From the very beginning NATO Council and in large part General Clark believed that in order to stop ethnic cleansing was to hit the Yugoslavian 3rd Army right in *Kosovo.* Of course, General Short, an Air Force officer, did not believe that. General Short told to John Tirpak:

"I never felt we were going to be able to stop ethnic cleansing, and in act we did not…Most of the damage had been done before we ever started attacking targets on the ground."

General Short believed that the way to force Milosevic's hand was not by mounting attacks but rather by an overall effort.

The classic strategic bombing effect started to being felt in *Belgrade* after two months of aerial attacks. *Belgrade* was without electricity for days, no fuel to keep the military running, infrastructure was systematically destroyed including bridges over the *Danube River*. That was the kind of strategic warfare that General Short believed in, it worked. In his words:

"I am quite frankly, a big fan of asymmetric warfare."

Asymmetric warfare is basically to cut the supply lines to the force that is feeding the enemy's units. An Army without logistics or cut-off from home can't fight (emphasis added).

On another note, General Short disagreement with NATO's initial actions had to do with the thousands of refugees scattered all over the battle field in *Kosovo.* According to Short, the presence of civilians on the battlefield, some of them used as human shields, led to inevitable bombing mistakes that killed civilians, Short said:

"There is little doubt in my mind that Milosevic had no compunction at all about putting IDPs inside of what we felt to be valid military targets…and in fact, a couple of times we struck those targets and then saw the results on CNN."

One of the obstacles to this air campaign was the North Atlantic Council, which consistently denied authorizing General Clark to draw plans for an invasion of *Kosovo* should one become necessary. General Short never received an order to wear down troops on the ground as a prelude for an invasion as it was done previously during *Desert Storm.* At this turning point of the war, when geopolitical factors intruded in military actions, General Short was given a free rein in trying to stop the genocide in *Kosovo* by going hard after *Belgrade*. Thus, becoming the most significant event in the air war. According to General Short:

"we made it very clear to him (Milosevic) that was exactly what we were doing…it would not be random bombing or demonstrating NATO's resolved."

General *Short's* view on flying high

There was a fundamental disagreement among NATO's high command as bombing altitudes were concerned. General Clark believed that by flying low, down in the trenches, could speed up the process of destroying tanks, armor and troops. But General Short was not an Army Field Commander, he was a pilot. And as such, knew better of the risks involved in doing that. Short's determination in avoiding losing pilots and airplanes together with his adamant opposition of General Clark's view preventing NATO from flying into a dead end. General Short convinced General Clark that parallel attacks an Air Force concept, could still be done attacking *Kosovo* and *Belgrade* at the same time. Flying low, on the other hand, could have exposed *NATO* aircraft to a variety of surface-to-air weapons, including shoulder mounted missiles. According to Short, after relentless suggestions to General Clark to switch tactics in *Kosovo*, Clark accepted the reasoning and released aircraft tied to *Kosovo* operations to attack targets in *Belgrade.* In this way, Short could use the precision strike aircraft like the B-2, F-117 attacking *Belgrade* and the lower technology A-10s, GR7s, and *Super Etendards* to hit ground targets in *Kosovo* making operations, according to Short, twenty four hours a day instead of night only. In this strategic line of bombing, Short believed that it could make civilians in *Belgrade* think twice about their leadership. However, the air forces were under constraint, according to *Short*, from conducting an air campaign, as professional airmen would have wanted to conduct it. One can wander, on that note, why *Milosevic's* government palace was not bombed. Given the opportunity, *Short* said, he would have arranged for the leaders of *Belgrade* to wake up after the first night to a smoking city. However, the supposedly accidental strike on the *Chinese* Embassy put a number of restrictions on what to bomb, on that note Short said:

"Toward the end of the air effort, we were restricted by enormous concern for collateral damage and unintended loss of civilian life…that was the litmus that we used to pick a target."

Of outmost geopolitical importance was the interference of the 19-member North Atlantic Council sensitive to human factors and the reluctant support and opposition of one council nation to attack targets as planned by military commanders. In that topic, Short declined to be more specific, according to *Air Force Magazine.*

The restriction of using air power, as stated by General Short, had to do with three measures of constraint stated by General Clark. The first, was to protect NATO forces in the theatre, including those in *Bosnia* as well as in *Albania* and *Macedonia*. The second was that the coalition holds together. Finally, "clearly", it was a goal for us not to lose any airplanes or pilots, Short said:

"I don't know any commander that doesn't enter a conflict with a goal of not losing any airplanes or pilots."

However, Short never expected to go into battle and not losing airplanes or pilots, even that did not change the way operations were conducted.

According to Short's assessment of the air campaign given to *Air Force Magazine,* General Short felt dissatisfied with the support from some nations to the overall effort. Short, in fact said that, there were European nations that failed to upgrade their equipment, especially nighttime capability or beyond-visual-range systems, were relegated to patrol missions only during daytime. General Short told John Tirpak during his interview that during the Combined Air Operations Center in Vicenza, Italy, it was clear "which allies were capable of going downtown on the first night and who wasn't. General Short praised nations like *The Netherlands* for keeping his aircraft updated. During the first night of the war, a Mig-29 was shot down by a Dutch F-16, Short noted.

General Short declined saying to *Air Force Magazine*, which nations were not capable and who was not willing to commit to the fight.

As a final note, General Short cited political constraints as the primary obstacle to air operations, he asserted:

"The political constraints made it very, very hard to conduct the operation…it was not just apparent at the three-star level that we were not following the classic air campaign that we all learned at Maxwell…it was highly frustrating that airpower was not being used as it could be and the way you have been taught to use it."

General Short also noted that the most frustrating aspect of the bombing campaign was that at a last minute, one or two countries could veto a target, causing airplanes already launched to be recalled. That represents a high risk for the air commander since he is sending pilots into harm's way if they are not going to drop, Short noted.

On the positive side, General Short mentioned the incredible success shown by Active duty, Reserve and Air National Guard in supporting the overall operation. Also Short asserted the importance of outstanding training of the U.S. armed forces, and the technology research invested during the last 15 years, thus making increasing the survivability and accuracy of the Air Force, he said:

"That made us a better Air Force, as we knew it would."

Chapter VII
Conclusions

The overall analysis of an air campaign can not be summarized solely by its effects on the battlefield or by the courage of the armed forces participating in it. There were other factors during operation *Allied Force* that limited the aerial bombardment, thus causing to extend the conflict, increase the casualties and jeopardize strategic alliances. The air war showed that NATO was not really prepared to deal with a major conflict in the *Balkans* region. It was not prepared politically as the North Atlantic Council was concerned and was not prepared military as NATO alliance was concerned. As a result Slobodan Milosevic tighten his grip on *Kosovo* committing most of the human atrocities during the early days of NATO's air campaign.

The initial, gradual and insufficient air strikes did not stop ethnic cleansing in *Kosovo*, thus allowing Milosevic to have a free rein in *Kosovo* to conduct his police action. History teaches us that gradual escalation of hostilities does not work, in fact we learned that in *Vietnam*. On the contrary, massive, and decisive strikes can initially produce more immediate and efficient results as proven by *Germany's Blitzkrieg* during the early days of *World War Two*.

The air campaign was plagued with geopolitical factors including media and public opinion, which exerted pressure on NATO to end the conflict as soon as possible.

In this sense, NATO had difficulty in dealing with issues that limited the use of decisive military force, something to be considered if NATO wants to survive in the 21st century.

Strategic Bombing

In the area of strategic bombing, the air campaign showed that there was little distinction between strategic attack and tactical attack. That could be explained in part according to how the air war is conducted, and what are its objectives. The strategic concept over *Kosovo* was further confused due to the tremendous political influence from NATO Council in selecting targets regardless of suggestions by U.S. and NATO military officials. On the one hand, General Wesley Clark believed in attacking troops and key targets in *Kosovo*. On the other hand, Lt. General Michael Short adamantly supported strategic bombing of *Yugoslavia's* main infrastructure, communications and supply lines to destroy *Serbian* economy. During the beginning of the air campaign, General Clark was forced to compromise with NATO political leaders on how to conduct the war, and what targets to hit thus totally conflicting with General Short's approach. As the air war escalated, it became obvious that, given the actual situation in *Kosovo*, General Short's approach made more sense. It was actually Short's approach that helped NATO win its day. Nonetheless, the classic definition of strategic and tactical bombing blended into one as bombers attacked tactical objectives and tactical fighters attack strategic objectives. However, General Short's approach to the campaign was strategic in nature, it went far beyond the initial interdiction bombing suggested by General Clark, it destroyed major area targets of high military value like production plants, military headquarters and fuel depots, facilities at airfields, and major communications and supply targets like rail marshaling depots, transportation centers, multi-tank fuel depots, and *Yugoslavia's* electrical power system. NATO's airstrikes in both the strategic and interdiction role produced considerable casualties to the enemy. However, all the strikes were conducted under strict political constraints, thus the exact level of physical damage inflicted on *Serbian* troops was difficult to assess. According to Pentagon planners, there are other ways to fly tactical missions. NATO planners said that tactical missions could have been flown the way the U.S. Navy or Marine Corps and possible other allies flew them, that is simpler and leaner missions. The U.S. Navy reported that it was able to fly many missions in the ground support role with much simpler and more flexible tasking orders (ATOs). This issue of sophistication versus simplification was a factor that delayed and jeopardized NATO key strikes over *Kosovo*. In the end the strategic campaign was successful, it was effective in many ways and it was difficult to provide evidence to validate its outcome. How effective it was depends largely on its results, Slobodan Milosevic lost *Kosovo*.

The Commitment Issue

One factor that really hindered the effective operation of the allied air forces was the level of commitment from NATO members. That alone is enough to conduct a research of its own including its history, the role of the U.S. and national security issues. More important than the military involvement was the political involvement. *France* concerns had a major impact on air operations; they altered key aspects of NATO's strike plans. Prime Minister Blair was reported to have asked for a veto on all B-52 strikes off from *Britain*. *French* influence added to *Italian* and *Greek* concerns led to the creation of a de facto *British, French, German, Italian* and U.S. management committee in which faced *French* and *Italian* resistance. The ambiguous *Geneva Convention* prohibits bombing of civilian targets or dual military-civilian targets if loss of life is at stake, thus leaving no room for military planning in an air campaign.

There is a tendency in any research to go beyond the specific issues at hand and possible to draw conclusions on facts and figures of air strikes and military technology without examining their interrelationships with political scenarios. But up to this point, the research described unclassified military issues whose answers can be used to improve or to train future military leaders only. The success of the air campaign over *Kosovo* has advocates of the air war and critics on political issues. There was no doubt that the success over *Kosovo* depended largely on U.S. missile technology, advances in target acquisition, intelligence reports, battle management, precision guided munitions and stealth penetration capability. The air war over *Kosovo* proved beyond doubt the capability of technology in weighing heavily on the outcome of the war. However the lesson learned is that neither the U.S. nor any other European power can afford to fight a major war by themselves. *Operation Allied Force* showed some shortcomings in equipment given to the *European* allies, lack of unity of command and probably control and communication problems resulting in a reduction of maximum effectiveness as NATO operations are concerned, as stated by NATO officials. Air Force sources stated that, the U.S. for example, learned a valuable lesson from European experience with the

CL-289 UAV, and BL-775 cluster bomb. At the same time, the USAF is looking into ways of interacting U.S. F-16s with those of *European* nations like the F-16AM in mid-life Update Programs. However, the USAF pointed out that this program is beyond many NATO countries financial capabilities and whether they are willing to commit to it remains only on paper. Government figures show that the U.S. spent some $36 billion a year on research and development while European nations spent another $10 billion on largely uncoordinated and often parallel efforts, a recurrent problem since the *Gulf War.*

Technically speaking, in the case of the F-16, *Kosovo* demonstrated the value of such efforts to upgrade the F-16 in strike missions and possible for improved on-board data links for targeting and battle damage assessment, and better avionics for targeting at altitude above 12,000 feet and in poor weather. At the same time, it was clear that the U.S. Navy and Marine Corps have the same need as the USAF to re-examine their overall modernization plan. According to military analysts, the plan is to develop a real world plan for modernizing the F-14 and F-18, deploying the F-18E/F and acquiring the *JSF.* On the USAF side, while the F-117 seemed to preserve a high degree of stealth, the lesson from *Kosovo* was that the strike-attack capability of the F-22 and *JSF* could supplement or replace that of the F-117 in the attack role.

Air delivery weapons and cruise missiles, according to Anthony Cordesman from the Center for Strategic and International Studies, were equally important for NATO allied forces. In the area of development, *Britain* and *France*, had not plans for the early purchase of *GPS-guided* munitions before the campaign in *Kosovo*.

Aerial Weaponry and Intelligence

One of the air-delivery weapons that caused concerns during the operation was the use of the anti-radiation missile and targeting systems. The anti-radiation missile relies on a radar signature, if the targeted radar is turned off the missile could easily miss the target. Newer technology in this area, according to Air Force sources, is the *DARPA Advanced Targeting Technology System* that may produce improvements in targeting that allow *HARM* missiles to target even short emissions of radar signature. Similarly, the enhancement of the *HARM* targeting systems may provide enough accuracy to allow the use of an area attack weapon like the AGM-154A *Joint Stand-Off Weapon (JSOW)* against SAMs, or air defense radar/command and control sites. Military analysts like Anthony Cordesman, raised serious questions about future air defense suppression missions, whether anti-radiation missiles can be counted on performing its mission and the need for systems that can target and destroy land-based air defense systems rather than simply suppress them.

The air war over *Kosovo* showed the need to have or to deploy in the future a system capable to rapidly deploy the intelligence, reconnaissance, targeting and battle assessment assets needed to get maximum benefit from both air power and long range land artillery systems, as analyzed by Anthony Cordesman. The USAF reported that the combination of *JSTARS*, the U-2, unmanned aerial vehicles (UAVs) and better satellite and reconnaissance coverage plus target analysis proved critical in giving attack sorties more lethality. According to Cordesman, the basic systems now seem to be in place to use air and missile power far more synergistically, but questions exist as to the adequacy of the current fleet, and as to the integration of national intelligence assets in supporting theatre operations.

The Air Force reported that the U.S. *Link 16* secure data-sharing system worked well, but was not disseminated widely enough, and the U.S. military services were not prepared to use it to pass on real-time command and targeting data efficiently. The USAF, according to Cordesman, was not allowed to use the *Joint TAC Info Distribution Systems (JTIDS)* to provide automated situational awareness data and have to rely on voice to provide situational data to allied aircraft. The J-8 *JSTARS* seemed to have made significant progress since the *Gulf War*, but the USAF is looking into its ability to characterized small military movements and adequately distinguish armor and artillery from other vehicles including data links to transmit data directly to attack aircraft. Military analysts believe that improvements in this area could help *JSTARS* avoid collateral damage and provide real time targeting data to use with standoff munitions.

In the area of military intelligence, some experts feel that national assets do not adequately support theatre commanders in terms of information, reaction times, link of information between agencies and adequate discrimination of classified material, and responsiveness to the theatre of operations. These problems, as stated by Cordesman, were major lessons of the *Gulf War* and *Kosovo* and could be used to study information flow to coalition allies, and the ability to maximize the interaction of data provided to NATO's Combined Air Operations Center *(CAOC)*. Some officials in the Department of Defense believe that the need to suddenly improvise a new integrated approach to communications and information to fight the air war in *Kosovo* illustrates the need for a broader Global Information Grid *(CIG)*. Also, the Air Force gained experience with *UAVs,* and with more sophisticated systems like *Helios 1* and *Mirages IVP, F1CR* and *Super Etendards* in the area of communications and improving interaction between operational and intelligence information.

As stated by General Clark, both targeting and battle damage assessment created major problems during the *Kosovo* campaign, severely challenging the credibility of my U.S. plans for information dominance, and at the same time, revolutionizing military affairs. In this area, Anthony Cordesman believes that, the present U.S. effort to substitute force quality for force numbers may be a little more than high technology wishful thinking. The lesson of *Kosovo* seemed to be that the U.S. cannot eliminate the enemy's ability to exploit asymmetric warfare and needs significant improvements in both technology and force numbers. However, the military approach to the issue is more optimistic. According to General John Jumper, then commander of *Allied Air Forces* in *Europe*, stressed these points and effectively called for a new level of real time situational awareness, mission flexibility, targeting and precision strike capability. These are particularly important in gathering targeting and intelligence data at low altitudes. Under poor weather conditions and at night the targeting and reconnaissance system with information provided by space-based and higher altitude sensor systems cannot gather or cannot provide sufficient real-time flexibility and resolution to minimize the risk of collateral damage. Thus, NATO and American forces could operate together and effectively if European nations build their defense systems paralleling those of the U.S.

General Wesley Clark, Supreme Allied Commander Europe, told the press that:

"We had a lack of ability in some cases to transfer information, some cases voice, some digital, beyond visual range, and identification of friend or foe."

And Defense Secretary Cohen said that:

"We found out during the Kosovo conflict that a number of countries did not have as secure communications as we want to have."

Political Geography

The air campaign over *Kosovo* raised a number of issues regarding maps and mapping. According to Air Force officials, the most politically sensitive was the need for up-to-date and accurate maps of all of key politically important facilities where collateral damage was a problem. This reinforced the need for comprehensive U.S. efforts to create a detailed topographic map of the entire earth for military purposes, as some analysts stated. This is the goal of the Shuttle Topographical Reconnaissance Mission *(SRTM)* which is a joint effort by NASA and the Department of Defense, including possible the CIA. The geographical survey is intended to create a topographic mosaic map of about 60% of the earth's surface with 30-meter resolution. It will cover the area between the latitudes of 60 degrees north and 56 degrees south, as reported by NASA.

Weapons Inventory

As stated previously, the data on U.S. and allied inventories of smart weapons and cruise missiles reported as uncertain by military analyst Anthony Cordesman, raised questions about whether the U.S. had more that a fraction of the inventories needed for more than one regional contingency. Pentagon reports on production of cruise missiles and guided munitions showed that only 200 *JDAM* kits a month were produced at the time the air campaign began. The number was raised by 500 a month by August 1999, and the goal was 700-1,500 per month, the actual Boeing production rate is 1,200 per month, as reported by Boeing Co. In the area of *Tomahawk* cruise missiles, additional Block III *TLAMs* will add up to 1,353 *Tactical Tomahawk* missiles for the Navy, with future plans to start acquiring them by 2003. It is being reported by Boeing Co. that it successfully tested and completed hard-target warheads for the *Tactical Tomahawk* and that it plans to convert about 322 additional *ALCMs* to *CALCMs* in light of the newer, longer range air-launched cruise missile.

During the *Kosovo* campaign, NATO ships and aircraft fired 329 cruise missiles during the first month of the campaign. The Pentagon did not report any breakdown in specific type of weapons used. An Air Force official reported that a total of 1,026 bombs were dropped, including 708 precision munitions and 318 non-precision munitions. Other sources reported that a total of 6,303 tons of munitions were dropped. Only 35 percent of the estimated 23,000 bombs and missiles used over the 78 day campaign were precision guided weapons, about four times as much as the ones used in *Desert Storm*. Anthony Cordesman, military analyst for *CSIS* stated that the U.S. faced growing constraints because it had only a limited number of advanced cruise missiles and *GPS* guided weapons, and allied air forces had even more restricted numbers of advanced guided weapons. However, Chris Hellman Senior Defense Research Analyst for *Weekly Defense Monitor* said that the Navy still had 1,000 *Tomahawk* left at the end of the conflict.

Other *Air Force* sources reported that running out of missiles during the campaign was not a factor. However, both Hellman and Cordesman concurred that *Kosovo* was not a major war by any means, but even placed limitations on some aspects of U.S. and NATO munition stocks. One issue posted by Cordesman, however is bound to be debatable within military circles is that weather imposed limitations of laser guided weapons and the weather-visibility limited most optical sensors. And by the fact that much of the target mix involved low-cost value military equipment with limited strategic and tactical value, simply does not make sense to fight a low-grade war with nothing but precision weapons.

Based on information reported by the Pentagon and Air Force sources, the *Predator* and *Hunter* unmanned aerial vehicles logged 2,000 flights hours in *Kosovo* and the *Hunter* about 900. Unmanned Aerial

Vehicles *(UAVs)* were a key tool in ensuring low altitude and poor weather reconnaissance and intelligence coverage. NATO reported that *France* and *Germany* logged some 180 *CL-289* flights over *Serbia* and 220 over *Bosnia*, and the *British* flew the *Phoenix* for 20 flights before the air campaign ended, beginning on June 6. According to Air Force sources, the *Marconi Phoenix* had been developed to locate and designate targets for the *British* multiple launch rocket system and AS90 self-propelled howitzer, and to be integrated into the *Ptarmigan* command control system and Battlefield Artillery Targeting Engagement System. Also this system is being adapted from land support to air support missions and targeting data for the *GR7 Harrier* jet. Targeting lasers were also fitted to three *Predators* on an experimental basis, with positive results in targeting laser-guided bombs.

On July 6, 1999 Defense Secretary William S. Cohen praised the success of the UAVs and called for a renewed commitment to the vehicles. The directive stated that:

"We are at a critical juncture in airborne reconnaissance…Technology, especially in the areas of sensors and processing, has moved forward at an amazing pace, and correspondingly, the demand for information has increased even more quickly. The opportunity is here to develop, acquire, and integrate unmanned reconnaissance capabilities into the force structure at a rapid, but prudent pace."

Weather

The weather in the Balkans and throughout Europe from the early spring to early July remains critical on continuous bases. That was really a problem for NATO planners since the weather over *Serbia*, really does not improve until July. The *Meteorological Institute* reports that *Belgrade* has the highest annual rainfall during June and according to NATO the weather during the first 47 days of the air campaign was favorable only in 6 days, marginal favorable in 14 days and unfavorable for another 6 days. This meant that NATO could fly only 650 sorties per day on a day with excellent weather. That was achieved on the 50th day of the war, May 13th, 1999. NATO reported that on a day with bad weather, however, strike sortie rate was reduced by 30-50% and stressed that weather was significantly important during the first month of the war. During the first 21 days of the air campaign, there were only seven favorable days and 10 days that allowed 50% of the strike sorties to take place. Lt. General Michael Short, NATO's joint force air commander for the *Balkans* region, said that:

"The weather, just kicked out butts for the first 45 days."

NATO also reported that this weather pattern placed heavy demands and constraints on Global Positioning Satellite *(GPS)* guided weapons like the Joint Direct Aerial Munition *(JDAM)* and the enhanced *Paveway III LGB*. The latter equipment, like the *Predator* with laser illuminators, could fly under the weather ceiling and illuminate the targets showing a pay-off in its investment. The overall weather factor meant that NATO averaged only 0.5 sorties per strike-attack aircraft per day, this means weather forced NATO to operate 39 out of 78 days during the campaign. During a speech conducted at the International Institute of Strategic Studies, Defense Secretary William Cohen succinctly resumed the weather situation as follows:

"…Belgrade's battle strategy included a deliberate and manufactured humanitarian crisis. We were carrying out this air campaign, under circumstances in which the weather certainly was hardly cooperating. Again, I'd have to point out that out of the 78 days of this air campaign, roughly 20 days were actually clear enough to allow the inhibited execution of that air campaign. So under extraordinary geographical limitations, environmental limitations, we also had to deal simultaneously with humanitarian disaster. Our forces had to cope with helping to bring resources and relief to nearly a million refugees who had been expelled from that country. And we had to reassure the fragile nations on the front line to prevent them from imploding under pressure, as Milosevic had intended."

Final Comments

On 20 June 1999, at 10:50 EST *Operation Allied Force* was officially terminated. This was in response to the departure of all *Federal Republic of Yugoslavia* military and police forces *(VJ/MUP)* from *Kosovo* in compliance with the Military Technical Agreement *(MTA)* that was signed by the Commander of *KFOR* and representatives of the *Yugoslavian* Government on 9 June 1999. The *NATO* Secretary General has suspended the allied air campaign on 10 June 1999, 10:00 PM EST. The multinational force that participated in the *NATO* effort to bring swift end to hostilities in *Yugoslavia* and against ethnic *Albanians* in *Kosovo* achieved the stopping of the *Serbian* offensive and the withdrawal of *Serbian* troops from *Kosovo*. Also it allowed NATO-led international peacekeeping force into *Kosovo* and the safe return of *Kosovar Albanian* refugees back to their homes.

About 22,200 U.S. Air Force, Army, Navy and Marine Corps service members assigned to the *United States European Command* supported this operation. Even though technology weighed heavily on the outcome of the conflict, the success of *Operation Allied Force* would have not been possible without the sacrifice, dedication, courage and determination of the men and women of the *United States Armed Forces* and its *European Allies*.

About the Author

Dr. Albert Atkins is an Adjunct Professor of Aeronautics with Embry-Riddle Aeronautical University, College of Career education. He holds several Federal Aviation Administration licenses including Airframe & Powerplant technician, Advanced Ground Instructor, Commercial Pilot, Flight Instructor with Instrument and Multiengine ratings. His education was obtained from the Argentinean Air Force (Aeronautics Technician), Pasadena City College, (Associate Degree Mechanical Design), National University (Bachelor's degree in Aviation Maintenance Management), (Masters in Education), (Masters in International Business), and Southern California University for Professional Studies, (Doctor in Engineering and technology Management). Dr. Atkins has twenty years experience in the aviation field, ten of which have been in aviation education field. He held several positions as Airframe inspector trainee under FAR's Part 121, FBO Manager, Human Resources Manager, Pilot Instructor and Maintenance Instructor under FAR's Part 141. He completed several courses in CRM (Cockpit Resource Management) with Flight Safety International and American Airlines. He is member of the B-52 Association, Royal Air Force Museum and Strategic Air Command Society.

Appendix A

NATO Air Strength in Mid-May 1999

Aircraft Mission	U.S Actual	Planned	Allied	Total Planned
Fighter/ Bomber	272	488	192	680
Support	246	358	63	421
Reconnaissance	27	30	19	49
Helicopters	100	106	3	109
Total	645	982	277	1259

Note: At the end of the conflict, the U.S. reported that it had about 650 aircraft committed to the NATO force.

Table 1. (Source, Center for Strategic and International Studies, Anthony H. Cordesman)

U.S. Actual Deployment

Aircraft   Type

F-15E Strike Eagle   air-to-ground attack aircraft
F-16 Fighting Falcon   multirole fighter
F-117 Nighthawk   stealth fighter/attack

F-14 Tomcat	fighter
FA-18 Hornet	strike fighter
B-52H Stratofortress	heavy bomber
B-1B Lancer	long range, multirole, heavy bomber
B-2 Spirit	stealth multirole heavy bomber
A-10 Thunderbolt II	close air support
AV-8B Harrier	close air support
KC-135 Stratotanker	tanker-refueler
KC-10A Extender	tanker-refueler
EA-6B Prowler	electronic warfare
AC-130H Hercules	intratheatre airlift
C-5A Galaxy	Intertheatre airlift
C-141 Starlifter	cargo and troop transport
C-17 Globemaster III	cargo and troop transport
E-8C Joint Stars	ground surveillance
RQ-1A Predator	airborne surveillance reconnaissance and target acquisition
Hunter	unmanned aerial vehicle, surveillance
AH-64A Apache	attack helicopter

Note: Precise data is not available on all the support and transport aircraft provided by other NATO countries

Table 2. (Source, Center for Strategic and International Studies, Anthony H. Cordesman).

Sorties Rate and Intensity

Date	Day	Avg. Sorties	Per Day	Attack	Support	Tanker A/C	Losses Pilot	Total
4/13	20			1687				5926
4/27	34	340	130				1	11574
5/6	43	395	132	5670				17000
5/9	46			4500				18000
5/10	47	404	135	6100				19000
5/19	56			5450(us)	9002(us)	7174(us)		22626
5/21	58	245						
5/22	59	652						
5/27				3600(us)	14150(us)			
				3350(eu)	6150(eu)			
5/31	68	800	500					31529
6/8	74							500
6/10	76	585						400

Note: Secretary of Defense William s. Cohen testified to the U.S. Armed Services Committee on July 20, 1999 that NATO had flown a total of 37,225 strike and support sorties.

Table 3. (Source, Center for Strategic and International Studies, Anthony H. Cordesman).

NATO participation in Operation Allied Force

Thirteen NATO countries contributed to Operation Allied Force. The countries included Belgium, Canada, Denmark, France, Germany, Italy, Netherlands, Norway, Portugal, Spain, Turkey, United Kingdom, and the United States.

Air Forces

COUNTRY	AIRCRAFT
BELGIUM	F-16
CANADA	CF-18
DENMARK	F-16A
FRNACE:	JAGUAR, MIRAGE 2000C, 2000D, F-1, MIR-IVP, JAG-A, E3-F, C-135F, UAV CL-289, UAV CR, PUMA SA-330, HORIZON, C-160, FS FOCH AIR WING, SUPER ETENDARD
GERMANY	TORNADO PA-200H, PA-200E, UAV CL-289

ITALY: TORNADO ADV, PA-2001, AMX, F-104, BOEING 707T AND AIRCRAFT ON ITS GARIBALDI, HARRIERS.

NETHERLANDS: F-16A, F-16AM, KDC-10

NATO: E-3A AEW

NORWAY: F-16A

PORTUGAL: F-16A

SPAIN: EF-18, KC-130, and CASA

TURKEY: TF-16C, F-16, and KC-135

UNITED KINGDOM: L-1011K, E3-D, GR-7, GR-1, VC-10, TRISTAR AND AIRCRAFT ON HMS INVENCIBLE, SEA HARRIERS

UNITED STATES: A-10, B-1B, B-2, B-52H, EA-6B, F-15E, F-16C, F/A-18, F-117, EC-130, KC-130, AC-130, MC-130, C-135, RC-135, KC-135, KC-10, MH-53J, MH-60G, E-8C, E-3B/C18.

Sources: www.afsouth.nato.int/detforce.com

Opposing Yugoslavian Forces

Ground Forces:	114,000 active-duty soldiers and 1,400 artillery pieces.
Anti-Aircraft Forces:	100 surface-to-air missiles: a mix of SA-2, SA-3, SA-6, SA-7, SA-9, SA-13, SA-14 and SA-16. 1850 air defense artillery pieces.
Air Forces:	240 combat aircraft, including MIG-12, MIG-29, and 48 attack helicopters
Mechanized Forces:	1,270 tanks, including T-72s, T-74s, T-55s and M-84s and 825 armored fighting vehicles.
Troops:	40,000 in and around Kosovo, including 96 tanks.

Source: www.defenselink.mil/specials/kosovo

Appendix B

Tools of War

RQ-I A Predator UA V

General Characteristics	Airborne Surveillance Reconnaissance
Primary Function:	and Target Acquisition General Atomics
Contractor:	Aeronautical Systems Incorporated
Power Plant:	Rotax 912 four-cylinder engine producing 81 horsepower
Length:	27 feet
Height:	6.9 feet
Weight:	950 lbs. empty, gross 2,250 lbs.
Wingspan:	48.7 feet
Speed:	up to 80 mph (70 knots)
Range:	up to 400 NM

Ceiling: up to 25,000 feet

Fuel Capacity: 665 lbs.

Payload: 450 lbs.
System Cost: $40 million (1997 dollars)

Inventory: Active force 5, ANG 0, Reserve 0

RQ-1A Predator UAV
Source Air Combat Command, Public Affairs CWice, May 1998.

GBU-16 *Guided Bomb Unit-Paveway II*

Specifications

Mission:	Air interdiction
Targets:	Mobile hard, fixed soft, fixed hard
Service:	Air Force, Navy
Program Status:	Operational
First capability:	1976
Guidance method:	Laser (man-in-the-loop)
Range:	8 NM
Circular error probable:	9 meters
Quantity:	Classified
Development cost:	Classified
Production cost:	Classified
Platforms:	A-6, A- 10, F- 14, F- 15, and F- 16, F/A- 18, F- I I I

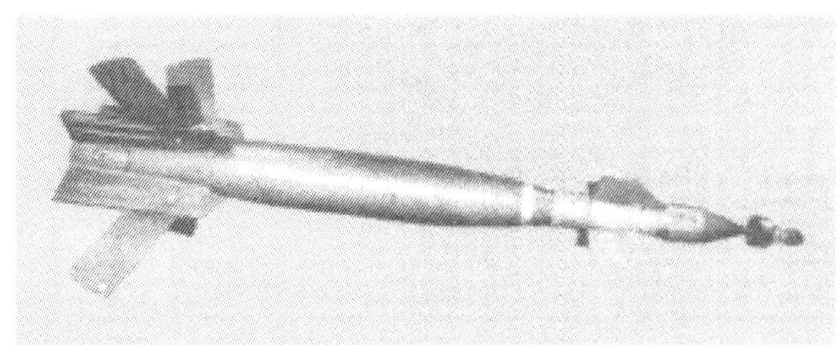

Source WWW.fas.orjzlmanldod-10]ls-vslsmartljzbu-]6htm

Dr. Albert Atkins

Joint Direct Attack Munition (JDAAp

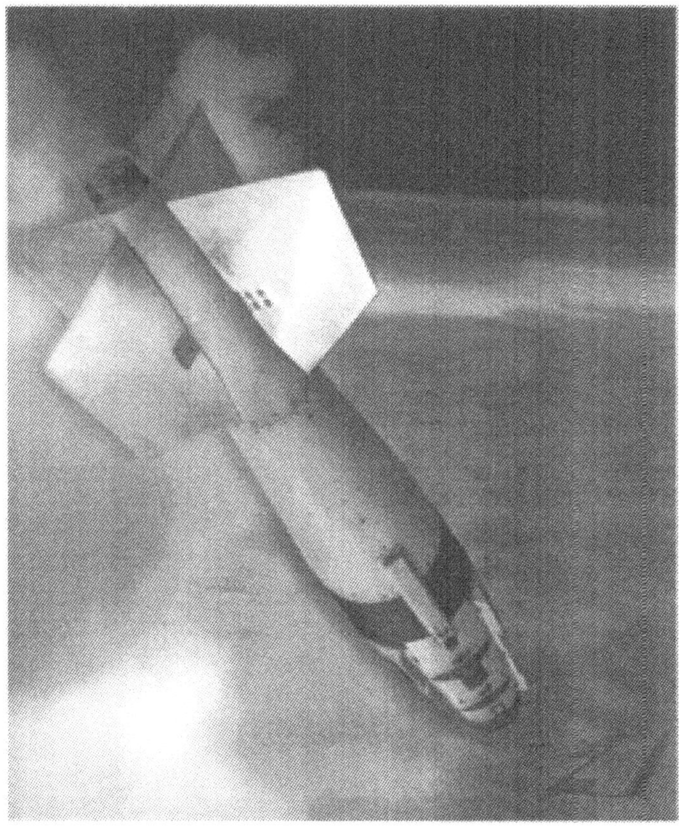

Boeing Photo
JDAM

Source Boeing Company

Tomahawk Cruise Missile

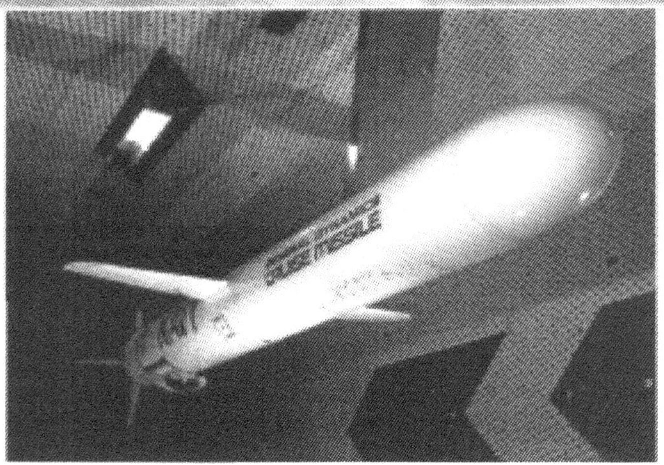

AEDC PHOTO 75-1551
Photo provided by Office ofPublic Affairs, Arnold AFB. AEDC Photo 75-1551

Appendix C

Cruise Missile Attack

Cruise missiles slammed into military targets from Belgrade to Montenegro, sent from ships and aircraft of the United States and other NATO nations.

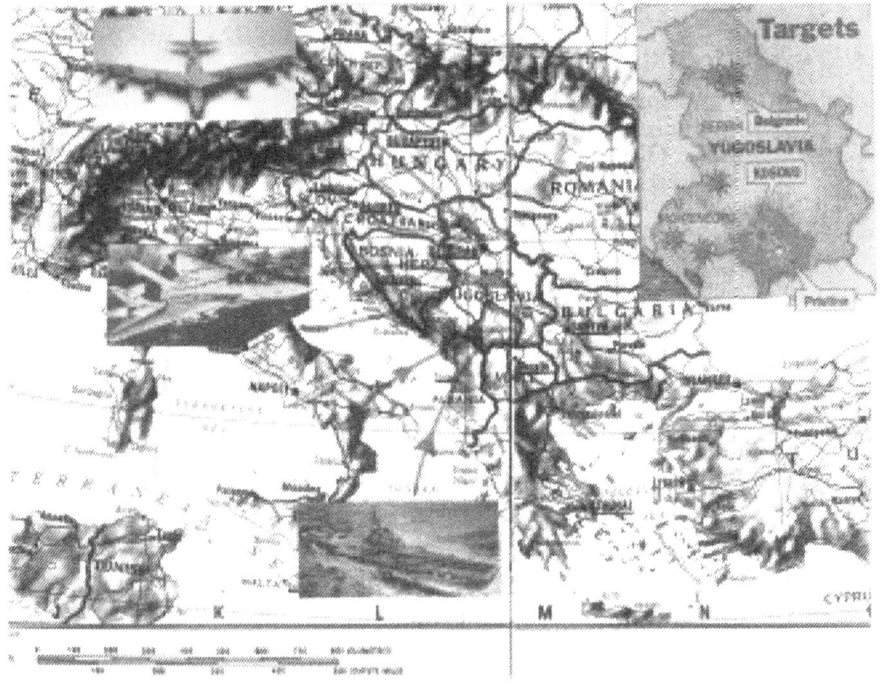

Source Victor Kotowitz, Los Angeles Times

NATO Damage to Serbian Army Military Infrastructure

Result: Reduced Serbian ability to sustain continuous combat operations

Source: Adaptedftom the Department of Defense press briefing, June 10, 1999.

NATO Damage to Serbian Air Force Capabilities

SA-3 Battalion Destroyed-1 (70%)

SA-6 Battery Destroyed-3 (100/6)

Mig-29 Destroyed-14 (86%)

SA-2 Battalion Destroyed-2/3

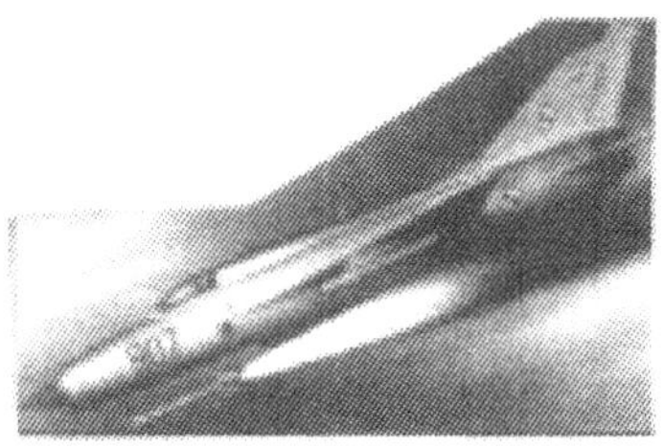

Mig-21 Destroyed - 24 (35%)-

Source: A dapledftom the Department of Defense press briefing June 10, 1999.

NATO Damage to Serbian Lines of Communication

Assessment: Moderate damage to lines of communication country-wide

Danube Bridges: 70% of roads hit, 50% of bridges hit

Source: Adaptedftom the Department of Defense press briefing, June 10, 1999.

Dr. Albert Atkins

NATO Damage to Serbian Electric Power Grid

Assessment: Military Operations, command, control, communications and logistics negatively impacted with power surges.

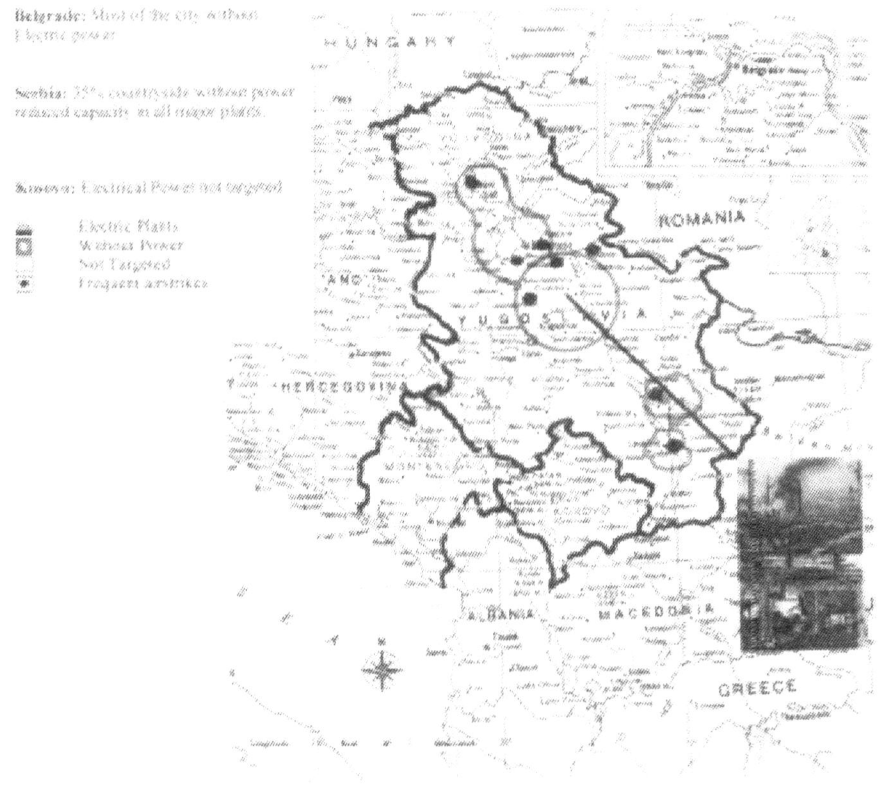

Source: Adaptedftom the Department of Defense press briefing, June 10, 1999.

NATO Damage to Serbian Defense Industry

Assessment: More than half of defense industry
damaged or destroyed.

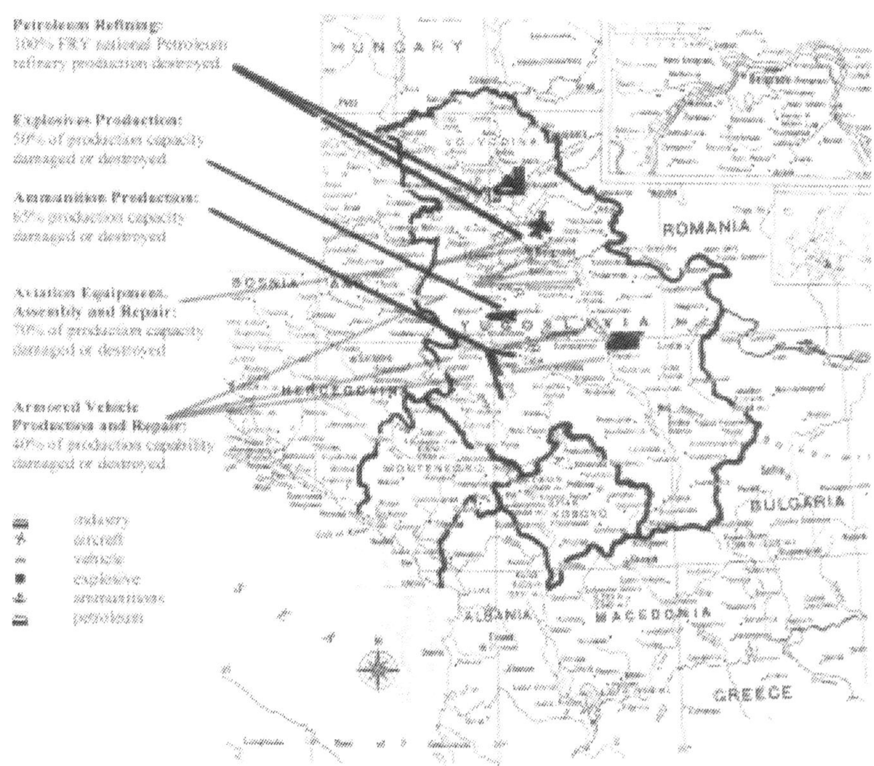

*Source: Adaptedftom the Department of Defense press hriefling, June
10, 1999.*

NATO Percentage of Total Strikes of Major target Groups, May 13, 1999

Source: NATO Briefing NATO Air Success as of April 13,1999

Source: NATO Briefing, April 13, 1999

NATO Total Sorties vs. Bombing Runs, April 13, 1999

Source: NATO Briefing, April 13, 1999 NATO Strike Aircraft Buildup

Source: Adapted from the department of Defense press briefing, June 10, 1999

NATO Combat Aircraft Involved in the Air War

Source: NATO Briefing June 10, 1999

SERBIAN Losses in Kosovo as of September 16, 1999

Source: Provided by Anthony H. Cordesman from data provided in the NATO briefing by SACEUR, General Wesley Clark, on September 16, 1999.

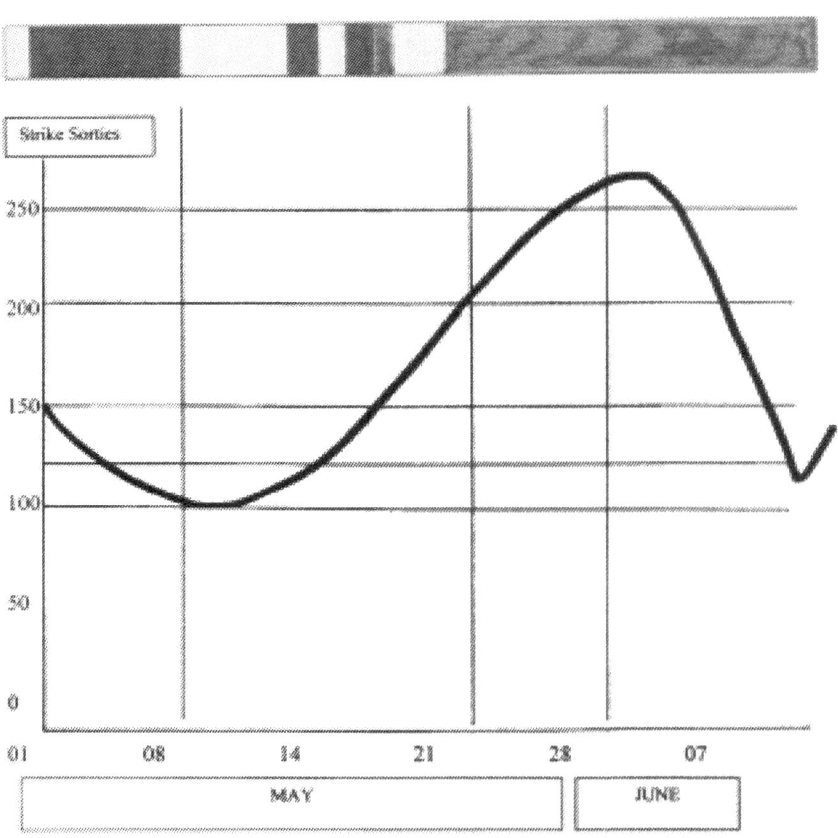

Source: Adaptedftom department of Defense press briefing June 10, 1999.

The Shift to an All Axis Attack

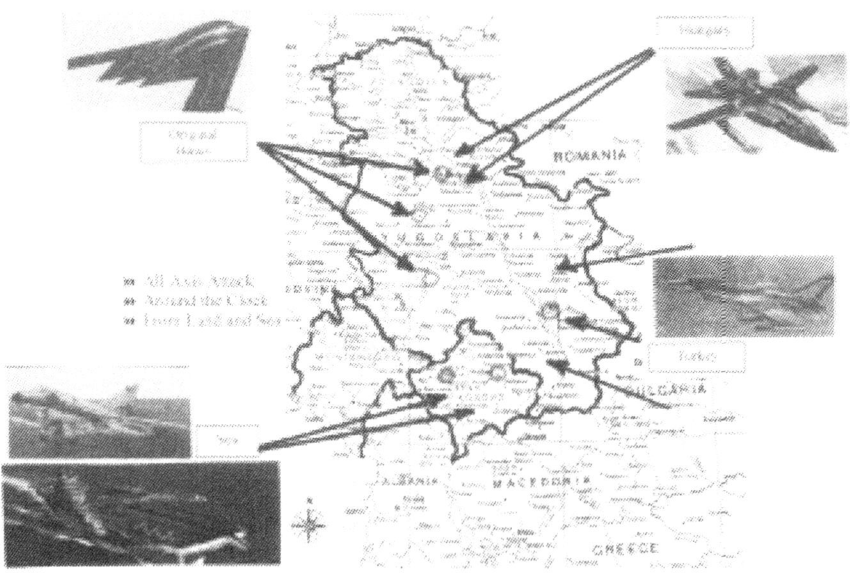

Source: Adaptedftom department of Defense press briefing June 10, 1999.

Serbian Forces Withdrawal Timetable

EIF + 1   10 JUNE
ZONE III (-) WITHDRAWAL

EIF + 6   15 JUNE
ZONE I WITHDRAWAL

OF +9   18 JUNE
ZONE I I WITHDRAWAL

ElF + 11   20 JUNE
ZONE III (+)

EIF+ 11   20 KNE
TOTAL WITHDRAWAL FROM KOSOVO

Source: Adaptedftom department of Defense press briefing June 10, 1999.

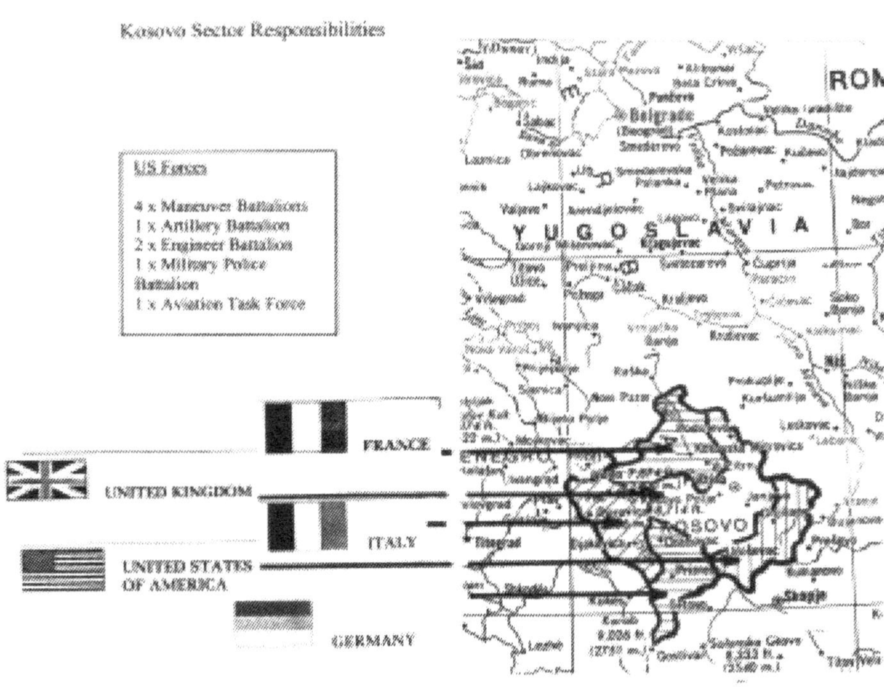

Source: Adaptedftom department of Defense press briefing June 10, 1999.

Bibliography

Air Combat Command, Predator UAV, Public Affairs Office, Langley AFB, VA., May 1998.

Military Analysis Network, *Guided Bomb Unit GBU-16*, www.fas.org/man/dod-101/sys/smart/gbu-16htm. October 1999.

Robert Algaretti, *Joint Direct Attack Munitions JDAM*, Boeing Co., www.boeing.com

Anthony H. Cordesman, *The War in Kosovo*, Center Strategic International Studies, Co-Director Middle East Program, September 1999.

Colonel Putt Richards Commander 163rd Air Refueling Wing, *Interview*, March ARB, CA. September 1999.

Colonel Jeffrey Holshouser, Commander 452nd Air Mobility Wing, *Interview*, March ARB, September 1999.

Air Combat Command, *Predator Fact Sheet*, www.acc.of.mil/public/html, September 1999.

Air Force South, *Operation Allied Force Background*, www.afsouth.nato.int/detforce/force.htm, September 1999.

Center for Defense Information, www.cdi.org/issues/europe/kosuforc3.html.

Defense Link, *Predator Demonstration over Kosovo,* www.defenselink.mil/specials/kosovo, September 1999.

Air Combat Command, www.acc.of.mil/public/library/html.

Defense Link, *Allied Air Missions Showing Results,* www.defenselink.mil/news/serb1999/html July 1999.

Joint Direct Attack Munitions, www.boeing.com/defesnse-space/missile/htm, October 1999.

www.dynamite.com.au/html

www.europeaninstitute.org/sum98.htm

Paul Richter, Staff Writer, *B-2 Drops Bad PR in Air War,* Los Angeles Times, July 1999.

www.mco.com/menu/archive/army/1999/htm

www.nato.int/kosovo/all-force.htm

Legal Bases for Operation Allied Force, www.mod.uk/news/kosovo/legal.htm September 1999.

Raids Against Chinese Embassy, www.chinanews.org/chinaembassy/htm

General Charles Horner USAF, Ret. *Interview,*www.abcnews.go.com/html, July 1999.

Richard N. Haas, *Modest Objectives, Ambitious Means,* www.brook.edu/views/html
www.cdi.org/weekly/html, Washington Post, July 1999.

Press Conference on Kosovo Strike
*Assessment,*www.eurocom.mil/operation/af/nato/1999/meabriefing.htm, *September 1999.*

Washington Watch, John A. Tirpak, Senior Editor, *Short's view of the Air Campaign,* Air Force Magazine, September 1999.

www.eucom.mil/operation/af/archive.html, September 1999.

www.serbia-info.com/news/1999-05/09/11685.1html, September 1999.

Jane's *All The World's Aircraft* 1996-1997

Federation of American Scientists, *"Military Airplanes"*, July 1999.